Jesus in our Western Culture

Jesus in our Western Culture

Mysticism, Ethics and Politics

Edward Schillebeeckx

SCM PRESS LTD

Translated by John Bowden from the Dutch
Als Politiek Niet Alles Is... Jesus in onze Westerse Cultuur,
published 1986 by Uitgeverij Ten Have, Baarn, Netherlands

©Uitgeverij Ten Have 1986

©Translation John Bowden 1987

British Library Cataloguing in Publication Data

Schillebeeckx, Edward
Jesus in our Western culture: mysticism,
ethics and politics.
1. Jesus Christ
I. Title   II. Als politick niet alles is.
English
232   BT304.97

ISBN 0–334–02098–0

First British edition published 1987
by SCM Press Ltd, 26-30 Tottenham Road, London N1 4BZ

Phototypeset by Serious Software Ltd
and printed in Great Britain by
Richard Clay (The Chaucer Press) Ltd, Bungay, Suffolk

Contents

Introduction

Abraham Kuyper died in 1920; at that time I was only a boy of six. He and I have in common that we are both honorary Doctors of the oldest university in the Netherlands, Leuven. I would like to express my warmest thanks to the Free University of Amsterdam and especially its Faculty of Religion for their magnificent gesture in inviting me to give the Abraham Kuyper lectures this year.

The only thing I remember from newspaper reports about the previous Kuyper lectures given by Rosemary R.Ruether, *To Change the World: Christology and Cultural Criticism*, published in English by SCM Press and Crossroad Publishing Company in 1980, is Dr Ruether's bold assertion that no theologian can be taken seriously unless he or she can cook. I can assure you that since then I have in fact got quite a reputation as a cook, so that may be my credentials for giving these Kuyper lectures.

In these lectures I want to talk about God – about God in his or her relationship to men and women and therefore about the mystical or theologal, the ethical and the political dimension of this belief in God, all viewed from the focal point of Jesus of Nazareth, whom the church confesses as the Christ. So in the Dutch edition I called these lectures: 'If politics is not everything . . .'

Men and women are the subject of Christian belief in God, but they are also cultural: they are cultural beings. Because of that the specific social and cultural context in which believers live, that on which Christian faith is in fact modelled, is at the same time that through which this faith is assimilated in a living way and finally that in which faith is experienced in concrete terms by men and women living here and now. Although this culture with its personal and socio-political ethics is 'sovereign in its own sphere', as Abraham Kuyper used to put it, belief in God also stands in a critical relationship to any culture, and moreover this culture is prepared, by the grace which calls men and women to act, for eternal life for them. The gospel of Jesus Christ is ultimately concerned with the messianic preparation of our world to become the kingdom of God. Therefore in the English version I have chosen for these Kuyper lectures the somewhat general title *Jesus in our Western Culture*.

Amsterdam,   Edward Schillebeeckx
27-30 May 1986

1

Who or what brings salvation to men and women?
The world and God

It may be said to be an irony of history that the cultural forces which we have accumulated since the seventeenth century as the historical liberators of humanity, namely science and technology, which were suppose to free us from all those things from which religion was unable to free men and women – hunger and poverty, tyranny, war and historical fate – at present seem not only to have increased this hunger and poverty further and conjured up the possibility of a nuclear war but also – in human hands – to pose the greatest threat to our future.

From as early as the seventeenth century, but above all since the eighteenth century, science seemed to herald the end of all historical religions. These were – it was heedlessly thought – a phase of childish ignorance in human history. Now that we are approaching the year 2000 it is precisely science and technology which are posing 'the religious question' to us more urgently than ever, at least where the question of human meaning still has any significance. Scientific theories are now seeking the fundamental condition for the possibility of science itself, and this lies outside or beyond all the sciences. It is not the sciences or technology that instil anxiety into us, but their claim to provide absolute salvation. At any rate we are coming to the conclusion that human, scientific and technological creativity carries within itself the possibility of self-destruction. Science and technology, once hailed as liberators of humanity, have subjected men and women to a new kind of fate which brings social and historical slavery. Is it possible that our human creativity itself is threatening the very meaning of our history? Will the 'guardian of creation' (Gen.2.15; 1.28) become its betrayer? Or, can a finite being ever be understood and liberated in its own terms? Is not a recognized and living relationship to 'the transcendent' (He? She? or It?) part of the unfathomable ground of our human creativity and therefore part of the deepest and ultimate inspiration of all humanism?

Talk about God is at the same time talk about the salvation of human beings

Theology, talk about God, is more than christology; in other words, while as Christians we can and may make Jesus the Christ the centre of history for ourselves, we are not at the same time in a position to argue that the historical revelation of salvation from God in Jesus Christ exhausts the question of God, nor do we need to. Although we cannot attain Jesus in his fullness unless at the same time we also take into account his unique relationship with God which has a special nature of its own, this does not of itself mean that Jesus' unique way of life is the only way to God. For even Jesus not only reveals God but also conceals him, since he appeared among us in non-godlike, creaturely humanity. As man he is a historical, contingent being who in no way can represent the full riches of God . . . unless one denies the reality of his real humanity (and that runs counter to the consensus of the church). So the gospel itself

2

forbids us to speak of a Christian religious imperialism and exclusivism. Isaiah's prophetic complaint also applies to Jesus: 'Truly, you are a God who hides yourself' (Isa.45.15), and the Gospels make him say this on the cross.

On the other hand, anyone who does not take into account the specific and distinctive religious relationship of Jesus to this hidden God seeks to understand the historical Jesus either on the basis of pre-existing metaphysical concepts or within pre-existing social and political frameworks of interpretation, both of which are alien to the gospel. In both instances the contingent, historical figure of Jesus is distorted: so that he becomes either a politically neutral mystical figure who is alien to the world or a candidate of a political party (whether right- or left-wing) up for election. Here we are confronted with the difficult, almost paradoxical idea on the one hand of Jesus' particular, indescribably special relationship with God, and, on the other hand, with the fact that as a historical phenomenon he is a 'contingent event' which cannot exclude or deny other ways to God and therefore cannot annex ethics exclusively for himself. This also implies that we cannot reduce theology to a christology: there are questions and also religious problems which lie outside the christological field. That is very important for the ecumene of religions. At all events, while Jesus is a unique manifestation of God he is also a contingent one. Anyone who overlooks this fact of the concrete and specific humanity of Jesus, precisely in 'human' qualities which can be recognized in geographical and socio-cultural terms, makes the man Jesus a necessary divine emanation – and this goes against the deepest meaning of all the christological confessions and the very nature of God, as absolute freedom, and moreover essentially trivializes human ethics and the other religions and fails to take them seriously.

The consequence of the fact that God's creation is at the same time the beginning of the history of salvation and perdition is essentially that God has not revealed himself exclusively and exhaustively in Jesus Christ and therefore that when it comes to talking about God, any man or woman has a right to his or her say. Although talk about God cannot be reduced to talk about humanity, far less to ethical talk about humanity, talk about God is nevertheless indissolubly bound up with talk about men and women and the world in which they live. But in that case we can no longer go on talking about God in terms of function. We modern men and women can no longer think of God in terms of need and function, of importance, efficiency or utility for human beings. In this sense God transcends the category of necessity, utility and contingency. 'There was no need for God.' Even human beings who do not believe in God find their life in the world meaningful and exert themselves for a better and more human world. In this respect neither Christian believers nor non-believers have a greater wisdom or ... greater modesty *per se*. God is not to be reduced to a function of humanity, of society or of the world. For all this God is a useless, superfluous hypothesis. For us, God as a remedy for the human condition has completely disappeared from sight. The mayfly phenomenon of 'death of God' theology was nevertheless the modern result of our former cosmological and anthropocentric proofs of God. The gradual death of the old theism can be illuminated briefly and concisely.

In our time the old Greek and mediaeval starting point for arriving at God, namely the finitude of the universe, of the cosmos and human beings in it, will no longer

4

do. Finitude is now no longer the exclusively *religious* term that it used to be. At the very stage when he was a militant atheist Sartre made the most acute philosophical analyses of the finitude of humanity and the world. The denial of God no longer calls into being the boastful divinization of humanity, as it perhaps did even in the nineteenth century; on the contrary, it leaves men and women in their *condition humaine*, sometimes in a down-to-earth way, sometimes bravely or humbly.

The modern starting-point, namely human subjectivity, which posits God as the real condition of possibility, has also disappeared. At any rate no one prays to some 'condition of possibility' or another. Both the cosmic and the anthropocentric starting points thus assume that modern men and women do not need God to explain the cosmos; far less do they need God in order to establish a meaningful anthropology or ethics. But precisely in this Western social climate of secularization and religious indifference, of the spread of science, technology and instrumental thinking in terms of means to an end, the question of God becomes the freest and most gratuitous question that one can ask, and the way to God also becomes the freest career to choose. If within this context we look for points of expectation in human experience, echoes, traces or even held-back sounds which betray or suggest God's existence, his free presence within a hair's breadth of us, then in our time they might perhaps be found, be seen or heard, in the capacity of human beings to love without having a reason to; in that case we should perhaps have to look on the level of our human creativity, of feasts and celebrations, of generous self-giving and self-transcendence, though in the form of non-alienating self-emptying in favour of 'the other'. In such a context God would then be experienced by believers as pure gift, even pure freedom; every day new; without

5

any reason. God is not there as an 'explanation' but as a gift. The idea which people are so fond of these days, that God is 'the condition of the possibility' of human subjectivity, has taken not only the heart but also the 'logos' out of all belief in God and theology. By contrast the post-modern 'we do not need God' is precisely the supreme luxury of any human life. It is precisely that which a person 'needs'. Thus for believers God is the luxury of their life – our luxury, not so much our cause or our final goal, but sheer, superfluous luxury. The oppressiveness of a scientific technological society calls for such a God. In this sense God is more than necessary – but without becoming a function of our humanity. Therefore we also know ourselves called to a love which dares 'the useless', the superfluous, the unnecessary. It is a matter of our making clear to men and women something of God's completely gracious and saving, gratituous nearness which never leaves us in the lurch, not even when we leave him in the lurch. *Dieu a besoin des hommes*, God needs men and women, not in order to be God but in order to be a God of men and women. God himself determines in all freedom who he is and also who he wants to be for us. And on the basis of the Christian and religious tradition of experience we experience God as someone who opts for being as opposed to not-being, good as opposed to all evil. God is not on our side, as old political theologies often used to say; he is on the side of what is good, and that also means good for human beings. And it is important for us too to begin to stand on this side instead of taking God over.

Belief in God as the basis and source of free gift and freedom for the benefit of men and women as well within all kinds of wordly chances, determinations and indeterminacies is not a belief in the existence of God in the same way as people accept the existence of a distant solar system in the universe, about which, after all, we have no worries or care. It is a belief in God as luxury, well-being and salvation of and for men and women whom he has creatively brought to life on this earth as the treasured environment for human beings. From the beginning of creation God also began on the realization of salvation – including religious salvation – for human beings in our history. Belief in God is a belief in God's absolute saving presence among men and women in their history. In other words, no matter what the circumstances in which we find ourselves, even through what we human beings call sheer chance, determinism or our own fault, there is no situation in which God cannot be near to us and in which we cannot find him. The believer can even make sense of situations in which he or she truly experiences meaninglessness and absurdity, whereas the absurd remains absurd. That is in no way to say that the circumstances in which we may find ourselves in one way or another are the 'will of God'.

We cannot derive the active saving presence of God from our awareness or our experience of this presence which challenges us to make sense on our side. Nor can we reduce salvation from God to the particular places of salvation that we call religions or churches. Salvation history cannot be reduced to the history of religions or to the history of Judaism and Christianity. For the whole of secular history is itself already under the guidance of the liberating God of creation; and this transcends the local context, whether this is Asia Minor or centred on Europe. The first place where salvation or disaster is brought about is, moreover, our world-wide 'secular history', of which God is the liberating Creator – but also the verdict on the history of disaster which human beings have brought about.

7

Of course the absolute saving presence of God confessed
by believers is itself as such simply an offer and a gift;
by virtue of that fact it is not yet his presence, endorsed,
received and welcomed. No one is ever saved against
his or her own will. Salvation is always salvation which
is endorsed or appropriated as an experienced reality.
And some awareness always goes along with this appro-
priation. For although you cannot identify salvation
with the awareness of that salvation, you cannot just
separate the one from the other without further ado.
The content of consciousness, not the reality of salvation, was predominant in classical theology. Salvation
was seen as being realized directly by God's Word,
received in faith, bound to the proclamation of the
church, confessed in sacramental praxis. Faith, sacrament, church: these are the three essential elements of
all religions. But salvation here is and becomes a syn-
onym for religion; and this is a misunderstanding of the
experienced reality of salvation in the world. Talk about
religions and churches relates to 'second-order' statements; it does not relate to the direct, unedited first
realization of well-being and salvation, redemption and
liberation. The world and the human history in which
God wills to bring about salvation for men and women
are the basis of the whole reality of salvation: there
salvation is achieved in the first instance . . . or, indeed,
refused with consequent disaster. In this sense it is
true that there is no salvation, not even any religious
salvation, outside the human world. The world of
creation, our history within nature as an environment,
is the sphere of God's saving action in and through
human mediation. In it the history of religions appears
as one segment of this broader history. The religions
are the place where men and women become explicitly
aware of God's saving actions in our world-wide history
and in which this saving action within history calls

8

religions and religious salvation to life. Within secular ·
history, at any rate, it was possible for religions to come
into being and understand themselves as movements in
which there were many kinds of interpretative experiences of the well-being and the religious salvation that
God is concerned to bring about. How else could
religions have been able to come into being? Certainly
not as something that falls straight out of heaven!

It was the exclusivist coupling of salvation with
religion and the church instead of the recognition of a
deeper basis of the beginning of salvation from God in
the world – the association of salvation with the human
world – that often resulted in an intellectualistic, idealistic, sacramentalistic and Neoplatonic-hierarchical
view of God's system of salvation; at the same time
there was also a one-sided concentration of salvation on
inwardness. This view is moreover an obstacle both
to Christian ecumenism and to the ecumenism of all
religions and ultimately to the ecumenism of the whole
of humanity. Salvation history is thus not entirely the ·
same thing as the history of revelation; in this latter ·
salvation history becomes an experience of faith of ·
which there is explicit awareness and which is put into
words. Without universal salvation history a special
history of revelation like that in Israel and Jesus
becomes impossible.

Thus salvation from God comes about first of all in ·
the secular reality of history and not primarily in the ·
consciousness of believers who are aware of it. Cognitive ·
awareness of it is of course itself a separate gift, the
significance of which we must not underestimate. But
where good is promoted and evil is fought against for
the healing of humanity, this historical praxis in fact
confirms the nature of God – God as salvation for men
and women, the basis of universal hope – and people

moreover receive God's salvation: in and through a love which is put into practice. The history of human beings, the social life of human beings is the place where the cause of salvation or disaster is decided. In fact our history is a history of salvation and disaster. For Christians who believe in Jesus as the 'author of life' (Acts 3.15), the history of suffering culminates in the historical appearance of Jesus Christ in whom the greatest disaster – namely the condemnation of the one who is called by believers 'the author of life' – is changed, through the overwhelming power of God's sending of the Spirit to Jesus and through him to us, into the source of eternal life. Although the will to promote good has the last word, because of the wickedness of this world the actual praxis of doing good is in fact incorporated in a way of life in which at least empirically, as in the case of Jesus, suffering and injustice have the last word.

Meaningful human history, salvation history and the history of revelation

Facts only become history within a framework of meaning, in a tradition of interpreted facts. This is the first level of meaning: human liberation is achieved and also experienced there. Within a religious tradition of experience of belief in God that human element of liberation is interpreted on a second level of meaning: in relation to God. Believers then confess that God has brought about deliverance in and through human beings. The secular event becomes the material of the 'word of God'. In this sense revelation has a sacramental structure.

Thus the religious significance of a secular event presupposes a human significance; in other words the saving event is an event which liberates human beings.

10

Revelation presupposes a meaningful human event, an event which is already relevant in human terms without direct reference to God, *etsi deus non daretur*. What is decisive is doing good to bring about liberation, without which the giving of religious names becomes empty, hanging in the void as a superfluous superstructure which does not mean anything. No one can take up a position above the parties in the struggle for good and against evil, any more than God can reveal his own being in any human history. Only in a secular history where men and women are freed for unexpected true humanity can God reveal his own being. At all events, in this secular history there is also a good deal of history of suffering and disaster: God cannot reveal himself here except as a veto or a judgment. Believers see the countenance of God in the history of human liberation. Non-believers do not, but on the level of human liberation (the material of God's revelation) that event can be discussed by believers and unbelievers alike, and can be discussed in a common language. Later the significance of the the newness of the explicit nomenclature 'God as the heart and source of any movement of salvation' will emerge. At all events we can see large as life that belief in God does not in fact make Christians any more human than others. In human love which has a preference for the poor there is an implicit confirmation of what Christians call God's free being, unconditional love, love without conditions. A couple of images may clarify this structure of revelation.

We can still see from the book of Exodus what secular historical event underlies the Jewish confession of the exodus (Deut.26.5-9): Moses 'saw an Egyptian beating a Hebrew, one of his people' (Ex.2.11c); he 'looked on their burdens' (2.11b). Moses looked round, intervened and killed the Egyptian. This fact became known and Moses went underground. Eventually, in solidarity with

11

Moses, some Semitic tribes staged a revolt. They freed themselves from the Egyptians; what happened was a 'liberating event', the first that was also experienced vaguely in religious terms. This secular history, which was already vaguely experienced in religious terms, was (above all in the Deuteronomic tradition) 'reread' by YHWH believers and made into an explicit theme; it was interpreted as a particular 'saving event'. Believers in God arrived at the experiential insight that the Lord had saved the people from Egypt. Here the structure of salvation history and the history of revelation becomes clear. It becomes evident that speaking in the language of faith about God's action in history has an experiential basis in a very definite human appearance in the world and history within the natural course of determinations, indeterminacies and chance. For human talk about the transcendence of God has no other ground than our contingency – our changeable, precarious human history. Religious language with its own spirituality gets its material from our human experience of contingency as a possible (but never compulsive) 'deciphering' of deeper dimensions which can nevertheless be experienced.

But this Deuteronomistic interpretation of 'liberation' (and not of 'flight', as in another old tradition) is only one interpretation; other Old Testament traditions give a different religious account of the exodus. So here in fact we have search-patterns or religious models which direct the life of believers. But it is also utterly clear in the other interpretations that an event which makes sense in human terms underlies the religious experience.

As far as Jesus is concerned, too, one must first look for a human historical event that liberated men and women, brought them to themselves and opened them up towards their fellow men and women. For precisely

12

Who or what brings salvation to men and women?

all this was the medium in which followers of Jesus of Nazareth began to recognize the countenance of God and on that basis began to call Jesus Messiah and in a special way Son of God. Without Jesus' historical human career the whole of christology becomes an ideological superstructure. Without the substratum of 'human meaning' in the event of Jesus all religious meaning in him becomes incredible; only the human significance of a historical event can become material for 'supernatural' or religious meaning, for revelation. On the other hand, unless we also take into account the positive relationship of Jesus to God, above all his Abba experience, this human liberating event that Jesus is never leads to a liberating christology and soteriology. In that case there is a break between christology and ethics, between Christ mysticism and ethical commitment, both personal and political.

I have said that before there can be any question of a thematized interpretation of faith certain human events take place in our secular history which in and of themselves – i.e. still without explicit reference to any transcendent God – are experienced as being positive: meaningful events which bring human liberation. For Christians, in so far as it liberates men and women for true and good humanity in deep respect for one another, human history is God's saving history and is so independently of our being aware of this structure of salvation as grace; however, it is not so without the occurrence of conscious human liberation. Sometimes theologians seem to suggest that only an 'ontological unconscious' dimension is brought to 'consciousness' through revelation, as if salvation were a question of awareness or better knowledge. But it is not the case that a veiled, purely ontological relationship, namely to God, is simply translated by revelation into categories of consciousness. What is involved, rather, is the religious

13

significance of the conscious human action which heals, liberates and establishes communication. The interpretation of faith seeks to make clear what it means to speak in terms of God's saving promises about the problems of our everyday 'secular' world and society in so far as human beings are freed and achieve selfhood in it, are freed from themselves to be free in goodness and openness for others. For 'the human' is a medium of possible divine revelation.

Finally, in all this there is something else that we must not forget. Because God is God, because he is not part of our world and therefore not part of our development of this world, he cannot be confined or limited in any human liberation movement or liberation of self. He is indeed the source and the heart of all truly human movements of liberation and salvation, but he does not coincide with any particular historical liberating event, not even with the liberating exodus event of the Jewish people or the ministry of Jesus which created space, liberated men and women and forgave their sins. The name of God, for Christians symbolized in the name Jesus Christ, can be misused not only by oppressors but also by liberators. This is the proviso which follows from the 'divine way' in which he is a liberating God – liberating constantly by means of men and women, but at least in the end never in a purely human way.

2

The career of Jesus confessed
as the Christ

Originally the term 'Jesus Christ' was not a proper
name but a double name which at the same time
expresses a confession, namely the confession of the
earliest Jerusalem community: the crucified Jesus is
the promised Messiah, the eschatological anointed of
the Lord: 'God has made him Lord and Christ'
(Acts 2.36; see Rom.1.3-4). That 'Jesus Christ' is a
confessional name provides the basic structure of all
christology; this confession is the foundation and the
origin of the New Testament. Without this confession
we should never have heard of Jesus of Nazareth.
That Jesus thus became known in our history is
essentially also dependent on the Christian confession.
But in turn this confession points to a being from
our human history, Jesus of Nazareth. This confession
is as it is because Jesus of Nazareth was the sort of
person who could evoke it. All statements about
Jesus in the New Testament, even when they are
recollections of historical facts from the life of Jesus,
have a confessional character. People talk about Jesus
because they believe in him and not out of historical
interest. However, what is also important here is the
fact that this confession relates to a historical person,
from a quite specific situation in our history: Jesus of
Nazareth, no one else, and also not some mythical

being or other. Christology without a historical foundation is empty and impossible. In modern times this
reference to history is at the same time an expression
of Christian opposition to ideological misuse of the
name of Jesus Christ, for the church's use of the
name Christ is subject to the criticism of the name
Jesus, to the criticism of his message and the distinctive
nature of his career, which led to his death.

The God of Jesus

What Jesus said and did so that others began to experience decisive salvation in him, salvation from God,
ultimately raises the question, Who is he that he could
do such things? If he mediates to us a new relationship
to God and his kingdom it is obvious that people should
ask: What is his relationship to God? And what is God's
relationship to him?

It becomes clear from this that in his humanity Jesus
gets a name, i.e. is defined, in terms of his relationship
to God. In other words, the deepest being of Jesus lies
in his unique personal bond to God. Beyond question
our creaturely relationship to God is also essential for
the rest of us human beings. But this relationship does
not define our humanity in its humanness. Nothing, no
creature, escapes this relationship, but that does not
convey anything about its character. There is more to
Jesus than that. It is evident from the New Testament,
on the one hand that God can only be defined on the
basis of and in terms of the human career of Jesus, and
on the other hand that Jesus as a man can only be
defined in his full humanity in terms of his unique
relationship to God and human beings. God is thus very
much part of the definition of what and who the man
Jesus is.

However, God is greater than even his supreme,

decisive and definitive revelation of himself in the man Jesus – 'the Father is greater than I' (John 14.28). The manhood of Jesus thus points essentially to God and to the coming of the kingdom of God on which he himself staked his life, i.e. counted it as nothing. For Jesus God's cause – the kingdom of God as salvation of and for human beings – was of greater importance than his own life. This reference to God, whom Jesus called his Creator and Father, which so disregards his own person, contains the definition, the real significance of Jesus. For Christians Jesus (*a*) is therefore the decisive and definitive revelation of God and (*b*) precisely through this at the same time shows us what and how we human beings can, need to and really may be. Therefore any definition of the man Jesus in fact has to do with the being of God. In Jesus God reveals his own being by wanting to be salvation of and for human beings in him. To repeat what the church father Irenaeus said: (*a*) human salvation lies in the living God and (*b*) God's honour lies in the happiness, liberation and salvation or wholeness of humanity. In the man Jesus the revelation of the divine and the disclosure of true, good and really happy humanity coincide in one and the same person.

In the Christian creed of the churches this view of Jesus is set against the background of belief in God as creator of heaven and earth. Christian belief in creation means that God loves us without conditions or limits: undeservedly on our side, boundlessly. Creation is an action of God which on the one hand unconditionally gives us our finite, non-divine character, destined for true humanity, and on the other hand at the same time establishes God in disinterested love as our God: our salvation and happiness, the supreme content of true and good

17

humanity. God freely creates humanity for salvation and human happiness, but in this same action, in sovereign freedom, he seeks himself to be the deepest meaning, salvation and happiness of human life.

To dare to call human beings creatively to life is from the divine perspective a motion of trust in humanity and our history, without seeking any conditions or guarantees from the human side. Creation is a blank cheque to which only God himself stands guarantor. It is a vote of confidence which gives the person who believes in the creator God the courage to believe in word and deed that the kingdom of God, i.e. truly human salvation, well-being and happiness, despite many experiences of disaster, is in fact in the making for humanity, in the power of God's creation which summons men and women to realize it. Therefore God, the one who may be trusted, is, in all his absolute divine freedom, a constant surprise for humanity: 'He is the one who was and is to come' (Rev.1.8; 4.8). By creating God takes the side of all that is created, all that is vulnerable. For anyone in the Judaeo-Christian tradition who believes in the living God, the cause of humanity is the cause of God himself, without there being any less responsibility among men and women for their own history.

The article in the creed, 'I believe in God, maker of heaven and earth and in Jesus the Christ', thus means that for the non-divine, for the vulnerable, God's nature is liberating love in Jesus Christ. God, the creator, the one who can be trusted, is love that liberates humanity, in a way which fulfils and transcends all human, personal, social and political expectations. Christians have learned all this by experience from Jesus' career: from his message and his life-style which matched it, from the specific circumstances of his death, and finally from the apostolic witness of his resurrection from the dead.

18

Jesus' career

'Kingdom of God', a key term in the message of Jeuss, is the biblical expression for the nature of God – unconditional and liberating sovereign love – in so far as this comes to fruition in the lives of men and women who do God's will, and is manifested in them. The kingdom of God is a new relationship of human beings to God, with as its tangible and visible side a new type of liberating relationship between men and women, within a peaceful, reconciled society. What that means in specific terms transcends our human power of imagination. We get a vague idea of it on the one hand through human experiences of goodness, meaning and love and on the other hand as it is reflected by situations in which we experience that the human in us, personally and in society, is threatened, enslaved and obscured so that we rebel against them. But these experiences only stand out against the background of Jesus' career. In it we have a telling vision of what the kingdom of God can be. The New Testament has demonstrated this in one of its earliest recollections when it says that with Jesus the kingdom of God comes close to us (Mark 1.15; Luke 11.20; see Matt.3.2; 4.17; 10.7). Belief in Jesus as the Christ means at its deepest a recognition in confession and action that Jesus has a permanent and decisive significance in the approach of the kingdom of God and thus in the all-embracing healing and making whole of humanity. It is essentially a matter of the distinctive, unique relationship of Jesus to the coming kingdom of God as salvation for men and women. That with the coming of Jesus God comes within a hair's breadth of us is a basic Christian conviction which therefore must be expressed in one way or another in the Christian creed.

The kingdom of God is a new world of suffering

19

removed, a world of completely whole or healed men and women in a society where master-servant relationships no longer prevail, quite different from life under Roman occupation. Precisely at this point Jesus turns especially to the poor. 'Salvation is proclaimed to the poor.' To a great degree Jesus' action consisted in establishing social communication, opening up communication above all where excommunication, expulsion, was officially the order of the day, in respect of public sinners, toll collectors who made themselves rich at the expense of the poor, lepers, and so on, everything and everyone who were 'unclean'. These in particular are the ones whom Jesus sought out, and he ate with them. In all this Jesus was aware that he was acting as God would do. He translates God's action for men and women. The parables tell of the one lost sheep, a lost coin, a lost son. To fellow-Jews who are irritated at his dealings with impure people Jesus wants to make clear through his action that God turns to lost and vulnerable men and women: Jesus acts as God acts. So he embodies a claim that in his actions and words God himself is present. To act as Jesus does is praxis of the kingdom of God and also shows what the kingdom of God is: salvation for men and women. Alongside Jesus' proclamation is his action, including the New Testament miracles. Historically there can be no doubt that in Jesus' time and in the early church religious preachers could achieve phenomena which in the judgment of their contemporaries were miracles. The individual stories in the New Testament reflect the consciousness of the narrators that Jesus was performing miracles, even if they expressed this in forms which do not correspond to our understanding of this event. It is certain that in his company they experienced a fullness of life of a kind which immeasurably transcended their daily experiences. In this context the miracles were

signs of the 'whole' or complete world of the kingdom
of God which was made present in them. Moreover, the
proclamation of the nearness of the kingdom of God
and the miracles of Jesus belong indissolubly together.
That the activity of Jesus which brought healing and
restoration and the whole of his life-style which freed
men and women from distress and misery were part of
his ministry is also shown by the fact that Jesus does not
just send out his disciples with the command to proclaim
his message of the forgiveness of sins and eternal life,
in short the message of the kingdom of God, but also
enjoins them to heal and restore people (see Mark
3.14-16; 6.7ff.). The people who could experience this
salvation from God in Jesus are also themselves called
to carry on the work after Jesus, indeed to a still greater
degree (John 14.12), in unconditional love for their
fellow men and women. The foundation of the life-style
of Jesus' disciples lies in the life-style which Jesus himself
followed.

What is therefore particularly striking in Jesus' career
is the essential relationship between the person of Jesus
and his message of the approach of the kingdom of
God. There is an inner connection between message
and proclaimer, as there is an inner connection between
this message and the action of Jesus which matches it.
With his person, his message and his life-style Jesus
stands guarantor for the liberating God who loves men
and women. From Jesus' career it becomes clear to the
believer that the God of Jesus, the God of Israel, accepts
the whole person and tries to renew him or her in the
acceptance in relationship to themselves and others, in
a world in which it is good for men and women to live.

All this of course presupposes that Jesus himself
also lived from the conviction of being endorsed and
recognized by God. The Christian tradition later formu-
lated this in a sharper form of words in its confession

of faith that the relationship between Jesus and God is that between son and father: he is Son of God. But what makes it possible for the church to use this name is the historical reality of Jesus himself, above all his Abba experience, which, in contrast to what he experienced in 'this world', was the source of his message and life-style, his turning towards those who suffered. Jesus' message of and about God was so integrated into his active dealings with his fellow men and women, which brought liberation and opened up communication, that his proclamation and life-style mutually interpreted each other, at the same time changing and renewing people, making men and women free for fellow human beings in love in solidarity, just as after his liberating encounter with Jesus, Zacchaeus, the toll collector, shared his possessions with the poor. By turning both to the rich toll collectors, the outcast, and to vulnerable children, the sick or the possessed, the crippled and the poor, Jesus makes directly visible what he is talking about; and so here and now he anticipates eschatological salvation: the kingdom of God.

The death of Jesus

Although he expounded the Law even more strictly than the Pharisees as the will of God for the benefit of men and women, the proclamation of the itinerant teacher whom people called rabbi did not fail to affect Herod Antipas and the priestly authorities. The tradition according to which Simon, a Pharisee, warned Jesus of the danger which he ran from Herod (Luke 13.31) is particularly credible in historical terms, above all because after 70 many New Testament texts tend to have an anti-Pharisaic tendency. In any case, at a particular moment Jesus came to realize as a result of a variety of events that his life, too, like that of John

22

the Baptist, would have to go through an ignominious death of rejection. In one way or another, perhaps in the dark night of faith, but in awareness of his task, Jesus related his approaching death to his proclamation of the kingdom of God. Despite the threat of death he remained faithful to his message and at a festive meal he bade farewell to his followers. 'From now on I shall not drink of the fruit of the vine until the kingdom of God comes' (Luke 22.18), After that he was executed, crucified by the Romans 'under Pontius Pilate'; there is good reason why that stands in the Christian creed. This, too, is in every respect also a 'political factor'.

Jesus' death, too, must not be isolated from the context of his career, his message and his life-style: otherwise we make the redemptive significance of this death a myth. It is precisely when we leave aside Jesus' message and the career which led to his death that we conceal the saving significance of that death. The death of Jesus is the historical expression of the unconditional character of his proclamation and life-style, in which their fatal consequences for his life pale into insignificance. Jesus' death was suffering through and for others as the unconditional validity of a praxis of doing good and opposing evil and suffering. So we must take the life and death of Jesus as a single entity; we cannot see the significance of his death in isolation. To give one's life for others is indeed the greatest sign of love and friendship, but only if any other solution is specifically ruled out as being impossible! God, to whom according to Leviticus human sacrifices are an abomination (Lev.18.21-30; 20.1-5), did not bring Jesus to the cross. Human beings did that. Although God always comes in power, divine power does not use force, not even against people who crucify God's Christ. But the kingdom of God comes regardless, despite human misuse of power and human rejection of the kingdom of God.

23

In the Christian tradition the death of Jesus becomes a central theme, although in the New Testament there are a number of earlier strata in which no interpretation in faith of Jesus' crucifixion is given. However, one may say that the Christian proclamation of the saving significance of Jesus' crucifixion goes back to the basic tenor of Jesus' own proclamation. Jesus was opposed to the idea of a triumphalistic messiah. Only if the title messiah, anointed, is redefined can it be applied to Jesus. Jesus' crucifixion revises the term messiah: the crucified and rejected Jesus is the messiah. Like God, Jesus identifies himself by preference with outcast and rejected people, the unholy, so that he too is himself finally the rejected and outcast one. This identification is radical. So there is a continuity between the career of Jesus and his death, and because of this continuity the saving significance of Jesus comes to a climax in the crucifixion and does not lie in the crucifixion, taken in isolation.

The redefinition of both God and humanity which Jesus gave in and through his proclamation and way of behaving takes on its supreme and ultimate significance in his crucifixion: God is even present in human life where to human eyes he is absent. The vision of the kingdom of God, of a coming world in which the wolf lies down with the lamb and the child plays on the snake's hole, could also be misunderstood. Before Jesus' death it sounded like a triumph to the disciples, almost too good to be true. But through and as a result of Jesus' ministry they became wiser: where the good triumphs and suffering and injustice give way, God is confessed in practice. Indeed, but there is more; there is also something else: Jesus points out that salvation can also be achieved in suffering and resistance can be offered in an unjust execution. Jesus, who can pray so attractively to his Father for his kingdom to come by

24

men and women hallowing his name on earth, here and
now, doing his will like the angels who have always done
it in heaven, and who then prayed that his and our
Father should indeed exercise the threefold function
of a Jewish father, particularly in providing for the daily
needs of his children, forgiving them the evil that they
have done if they have treated anyone spitefully, and
finally protecting them against all evil, Jesus, who
prayed like this, experienced on the cross that even
his prayer was more like a solitary monologue than a
dialogue of statement and response. It was true even
for Jesus that anyone who truly seeks personal contact
with God gets the impression in prayer of only listening
to the quiet echo of his or her own voice. On the cross
Jesus shared in the brokenness of our world. This
means that in absolute freedom, from eternity, God
determines who and how he will be in his deepest being,
namely a God of human beings, an ally in our suffering
and our absurdity, an ally too in the good that we do.
In his own being he is also a God for us. I therefore no
longer see a place for the classical distinction between
'God in himself' and 'God for us'. In the New Testament
a theological redefinition of various concepts of God
takes place, and also a redefinition of humanity. God
accepts humanity without any conditions on the human
side, and precisely through this unconditional acceptance he transforms human beings and brings them to
repentance and renewal. Therefore the cross is also a
judgment on our autonomous views: on our way of
experiencing the significance of humanity and the being
of God. Here ultimately and definitively is revealed the
humanity of God, the heart of Jesus' message of the
kingdom of God. God who in the human world comes
into his own, so that men and women become whole
and happy, even through suffering. God does not
impose any conditions on us human beings, even on the

man Jesus, for his redemptive and liberating activity: 'God was in Jesus reconciling the world to himself' (II Cor.5.19). It was not God but men and women who delivered Jesus over to death, but this execution is at the same time the material of God's supreme self-revelation prepared through men and women, as is evident from New Testament faith in the resurrection of Jesus.

The resurrection of Jesus

Only a new action by God could link Jesus' historical life over the break represented by his death to 'the Christ of the church's belief', with the confession 'He is risen indeed'. In the resurrection from the dead God's eschatological action in respect of Jesus, the crucified one, becomes God's own judgment, and his evaluation of Jesus, his message, ministry and death become clear for the believer. Easter faith presupposes a new divine action towards the crucified Jesus. In the first instance this expresses the relationship of God to Jesus – in the reception and interpretation of Jesus' disciples. Paul understood this well when he observed to those in Corinth who explicitly denied the resurrection: 'Some people evidently have no sense of God' (I Cor.15.34). Therefore the reality of the resurrection, the only thing which calls resurrection faith to life, is the test of both the understanding of God proclaimed by Christ and our soteriological christology. In the resurrection God authenticates the person, the message and the whole career of Jesus. He sets his seal on and speaks out against what human beings did to Jesus.

Just as the death of Jesus cannot be detached from his life, so too his resurrection cannot be detached from his career and death. To extrapolate the death and resurrection of Jesus as the heart of the Christian message is ultimately to keep silent about the prophetic content of the whole of Jesus' career: that is a 'Pauline kerygma' without the four Gospels and Paul is canonical only in the New Testament as a whole.

First of all we must say that Christian resurrection faith is in fact a first evangelical evaluation of Jesus' life and crucifixion, especially the recognition of the intrinsic, irrevocable significance of the proclamation and praxis of the kingdom of God which nothing can undo. To remove this first dimension is to evacuate the resurrection faith of content. But this faith contains yet more. However, even this 'more' is connected with the life and death of Jesus. The resurrection of Jesus is in the second instance the break-through or manifestation of something that was already present in Jesus' life and death, viz., his communion of life or grace with the living God, a communion which could not be broken by death. Already on earth this living communion is the beginning of what is called 'eternal life'. But thirdly, in the resurrection there is also an aspect of divine correction; it is not simply the extension of Jesus' living communion with God (beyond death), but is in nucleus the installation of the kingdom of God: the exaltation and glorification of Jesus to God. 'I believe in Jesus, the Lord.'

Yet all this remains an abstraction, which is not even good theology, if we leave out the living 'spiritual' presence of Jesus in his church. Through and in this Christian belief in the resurrection of Jesus the crucified but risen Jesus remains at work in our history. Jesus' own resurrection, his sending of the Spirit, the coming into being of the Christian 'community of God' as the church of Christ which lives from the Spirit and the New Testament witness about all this, and thus also faith in the resurrection, define one another reciprocally, though the one cannot be identified with the other. One can say that the 'church of Christ' which came into being on the basis of the resurrection of Jesus is the deepest significance of 'the appearances of Jesus': in the church community 'assembled' in faith there appears, is present, the crucified but risen Jesus. Where the church of Jesus Christ is alive, lives in prayer and liberation in the footsteps of Jesus, resurrection faith does not experience any crisis. On the other hand I must say with all my heart: it is better not to think that God is true, better not to believe in eternal life, than to believe in a God who belittles, keeps down and humiliates men and women with an eye to a better hereafter. In the Christian gospel both 'God' and 'Jesus' gain a critical and productive, liberating power of their own. This criterion of 'humanizing' proclaimed by Jesus above all human expectations of the humanum which is desired and constantly threatened, this solemn sense of the humanity of man, our wholeness and soundness, as something which is close to God's heart, is not a reduction of the gospel. The gospel is good news not just about Jesus but about the God of Jesus, the maker of heaven and earth, the God of all men and women. The message of Jesus embraces the kingdom of God in all its height and depth, breadth and length; not just the forgiveness of sins and eternal life, although it also includes that, indeed it is above all about that. Ultimately Jesus proclaimed the absolute, freely given and effective nearness of the God who creates and brings salvation. We Christians learn to express stammeringly the content of what 'God' is and the content of what 'humanity' can be from the career of Jesus. But there is an evident difference of approach between bourgeois middle-class Christians – which is what all of us in the West have become – and Christians in the Third World. Here in the West we seek as Christians, theologians, to address modern secularized men and women in order to make this faith in Jesus Christ acceptable; Christians, theologians in the Third World,

on the other hand, address dehumanized people, non-
persons, who ask, rather, how one can believe in a good,
liberating God in a world of suffering and oppression.
I think that this last approach is closer to Jesus' concern than the first. I think that our Western theology
will have to combine both forms of concern if we are
not ultimately to land up with a Western theology of
emancipation which by-passes Christian belief and
christology.

Eschatological future

The indefinable element of the *humanum* which is
sought and constantly found in fragmentary form and
then comes under threat again, i.e. eschatological per-
fection and freedom, can only be expressed in symbolic
language: in speaking in parables and metaphors which
go further than the impoverishing sharpness of our
definitions. Three great metaphors, put into words in
many kinds of sounds and tongues in the Jewish and
Christian Bible, suggest to us the direction of what
humanity will eventually be:

(*a*) The definitive salvation or the radical liberation
of humanity to be a brotherly and sisterly society and
living community in which master-servant relationships
no longer prevail, pain and tears are wiped away and
forgotten, is called 'kingdom of God':

(*b*) The Christian tradition of faith terms the complete
salvation and happiness of the individual (called sarx,
body or flesh, in the Bible) within the perfect community 'the resurrection of the body', i.e. of the human
person including his or her human corporeality, corporeality as a visible orchestration, the distinctive
melody of a person which others enjoy;

(*c*) Finally, the consummation of the undamaged 'ecological milieu' which human beings need to live in is

suggested by the great metaphor of 'the new heaven and the new earth'.

These three metaphorical visions of the future envisaged by God for humanity therefore already orientate the action of Christians in the world, not in an indeterminate or undirected way, but in a very definite direction, namely that indicated by the dynamics of these three symbols: concern for a better society for all men and women, above all for the outcast and marginalized, those who are devastated: pastoral concern for communication as an unceasing social and cultural criticism where injustice is evident; concern for the human body, for human psychological and sociological health; concern too for the natural human environment; concern for the wholeness of Christian faith, hope and love; concern for meaningful liturgical prayer and for a meaningful sacrament; and finally concern for the individual pastorate, above all towards the lonely and those who 'no longer hope'. Christian spirituality derives both its power and its joy from this eschatological hope in which Christians do all this.

3

Jesus and the church of Christ

The church as an institution never exists for itself, although it has often forgotten this (as have many religions). For that very reason we must not say too much directly about the church. We need a bit of 'negative ecclesiology', church theology in the minor key, to achieve a healthy balance, in order to undo the centuries-long ecclesiocentrism of the empirical phenomenon of 'Christian faith' and indeed for God's sake, for the sake of Jesus the Christ and for the sake of humanity. And these three, God, Jesus Christ and humanity, are one in the sense that they can never be set over against one another or in competition with one another. Even sin hurts God only in his creatures: in human beings and in their creaturely world, in animals and plants, in their and our natural environment, in our society, in our heart, our inwardness and our being directed towards solidarity with our fellow human beings. From a theological point of view, to damage and harm this world is a sin against the creator of heaven and earth, against the one whom, under whatever name, many people call God: the mystery that has a passion for the wholeness of nature and history, of society and human beings among one another, however much this name is also obscured and sullied by the behaviour of those in many religions who claim to believe in God.

Here we must look at the church in a double perspective: first in respect of what was said in the first chapter, namely that God wants to make secular history in this world a salvation history through human mediation. What is the significance of the church within this salvation history? Secondly, the relationship of the church of Christ to Jesus of Nazareth. Finally I shall be talking about the church ecumene.

Church and world

In the first chapter I said that salvation from God comes about in the first place in the worldly reality of history and not primarily in religions or churches which bear witness to salvation from God. This has consequences for our understanding of what religions and churches are. Religions, churches, are not themselves salvation but a 'sacrament' of the salvation that God brings about in his created world through the mediation of men and women in very particular contexts in which they live. Precisely because people do not 'put the church in its place' and at the same time 'in the place where it belongs' and forget the basic event of the salvation which is achieved in the world, churches often become sectarian, clerical and apolitical – and thus in a veiled way are very political. Religions, churches, are of the order of 'signs', sacraments of salvation. They are the explicit identification and ultimate fulfilment of that salvation. Churches are the places where salvation from God is made a theme or put into words, confessed explicitly, proclaimed prophetically and celebrated liturgically. So there is an unbreakable connection between 'world' and 'religion'. At any rate there is a necessary identity between the unveiling and the veiling of God. Anyone who looks only at the veiling can in fact forget God, suppress him or even ignore him: religions, churches, are the *anamnesis*, i.e. the living

32

recollection among us, of this universal, 'tacit' but effective will to salvation and the absolute saving presence of God in the history of our world. By virtue of their religious word, their sacrament or ritual and their life-style, religions – synagogues and pagodas, mosques and churches – prevent the universal saving presence from being forgotten. The future of the churches therefore depends on their effective presence in the future of the world on the basis of a life with God. As a religion or church is by definition directed towards human history, towards what happens in our world, the churches have a wrong understanding of themselves (*a*) if they do not understand themselves in relation to the world events as they experience them and (*b*) if in their participatory and also interpretative relationship to world events they think that they can abandon specifically religious forms like confession, word and sacrament. If the churches thus have a political significance, this significance must find its basis in the mystical dimension of the church and not in secular power.

The condition in which 'church talk' about God becomes possible is thus the real appearance of God in the history of the world; but the veiling of this presence in our world makes religious and church talk necessary. The churches live from the salvation that God brings about in the world. Religions – Hinduism, Buddhism, Israel, Jesus, Islam and so on – are a segment of our human history and cannot be understood without this 'profane' history. The religious symbols of religions 'mediate' for the consciousness of believers this veiled presence of God in the world. For even for believers he remains the hidden God, the one who is veiled, even for the man Jesus of Nazareth. There is therefore a 'divine proviso' in respect of the phenomena both of the world and the church.

The church, religion, is a matter of welcoming in

33

gratitude the as it were anonymous, veiled and modest coming of God in the world. Confession and Word, sacrament and practice of faith, action to heal and to open up communication, in the footsteps of Jesus, do not make the experience of the world event superfluous, while the so-called worldy 'outside event' makes speaking in the language of faith and Christian praxis necessary. Precisely for this reason historical and also social and political praxis in the world cannot be separated from action in proclamation, pastorate and sacraments. To break this connection is to damage the inner structure of religion and church.

The confession of religious people and their leaders is therefore never autonomous talk but a gracious answer to that which precedes all talk of believers: God's creative action in history in and through human beings for their salvation. It is men and women, believers within a particular tradition of experience, who express this action of God, put it into words; only in this way can we speak of 'the word of God', and then we are right to do so. God himself is the pre-existing source of all our talk about God. We owe our confession about God to God who addresses himself to us. Therefore churches are also communities which speak to God: praying communities of faith and not just one or another action group, however praiseworthy. Their praxis is putting into action the story that they tell, above all in liturgy. It may also be said to be characteristic that Jesus who gave a face that could be seen by men and women to the universal will of the creator God for salvation in a unique way in his words and actions was condemned to the cross by a worldly, secular judgment. In this sense a historical, secular and political event is the central point of reference for the Christian churches, an event which these churches can rightly celebrate in their liturgy; at any rate they are the

34

celebrating 'sacrament' of the salvation that God
realizes in the world.

The church of Christ and Jesus of Nazareth

In the church of Christ we are concerned with the story
of a Jew who appeared in our human history and who
after his death was confessed by fervent followers as
'the Christ, God's only Son, our Lord'. In that story,
set down in writing for the first time in what Christians
call the New Testament, we read how particular people
reacted to the historical appearance of Jesus and how
as a result they began to lead a new, different life. Also,
how yet other people, in just as radical a reaction,
fiercely rejected the same Jesus and even removed him
from the scene by executing him. Through the New
Testament, as in a mirror, we can discover in essentials,
historically, who Jesus was, how he lived, and what
inspired him. For these church communities wanted to
follow in his footsteps. We have no writings, no direct
documents from him. Only in the reflection of his
followers do we get a profile, a portrait of Jesus. So
there is evidently a dialectical interaction between our
understanding of the historical Jesus and the faith and
praxis of 'the church of Christ'.

His later followers tried to understand for themselves
what Jesus had meant for his first disciples and also
what he meant and could mean here and now for their
own life. This first process of interpretation came about,
at least in part, in what we call the New Testament. It
is evident from the New Testament stories that what
arose out of Jesus' earthly life is of such a nature that
it calls for either radical discipleship or fierce rejection.

Moreover we note that the fall and rise of the whole
history of the church consists in a new discipleship of
Jesus or walking in Jesus' footsteps, and in a constant

ongoing process of interpretation in which Christians, constantly confronted afresh with other situations and problems in the church and in the world, in faithfulness to the tradition handed down, accept in faith and yet critically what previous generations passed on. The identity of the 'historical man Jesus' with 'the Christ of faith' or the Christ of the church is a basic affirmation of the New Testament. There are no exclusive alternatives. Certainly we have begun to see more clearly that at the same time they form a relationship in tension without which Christianity is not Christianity and the gospel is not the gospel. For Christians there is no Jesus without the church's confession of Christ, just as there is no church confession without the liberating appearance of the historical Jesus of Nazareth.

The clear break between the 'historical Jesus' and the 'church's Christ' which many people have noted is therefore not so much the result of the modern historical-critical method as of the church's loss of its grip or influence on society and culture. Precisely by virtue of this emancipation the historical-critical method got its chance; before that church confessional interpretation of scripture had a monopoly. A scientific study of scripture is possible which is not under the control of the church; that is clearly an evident achievement of critical exegesis, which studies the Bible as literature, accessible to anyone at all. To begin with, the churches reacted fiercely to scientific exegesis because this demonstrated a break between Jesus as reconstructed by the historical-critical method and the Jesus whom the churches confess. This difference cannot be denied or smoothed over, not even if one can already discover in the New Testament a low implicit christology during Jesus' life, in other words before his death and resurrection. On the basis of the rationalism in the rise of historicist positivism the historical-critical

method did in fact react critically against the church's
tradition, in favour of a negation of the church's Christ
of faith. But on the other hand it revealed a distinctive
latent structure in all christology. The modern fact of
the free scientific exegesis of the New Testament texts
has revealed a latent, underivable structure of christology: the 'tension' between the actual career of Jesus as
this is witnessed to by the four Gospels, and the honorific titles given to him, which are confessed in the
same Gospels. I myself have already stressed that the
significance of Jesus must not be interpreted from these
honorific titles but from his specific career as a result
of which all existing honorific titles were 'broken'. The
tension between Jesus and Christ is not the result of the
modern historical-critical approach but is structurally
peculiar to the New Testament and to all christology,
in the sense that the distinctive kind of 'otherness',
indissolubly bound up with any historical and therefore
contingent reality, makes different interpretations of
the figure of Jesus Christ possible and necessary. On
the basis of this tension between the Jesus of history
and the Christ of faith no one can claim Jesus for
himself. It has been noted that the historical-critical
methods only become subversive of the church's faith
because their method is free of any authoritarian pressure. This therefore also makes the Christian churches
themselves favour the historical-critical method, but in
an apologetic sense. It was thought that historical
studies could demonstrate the continuity between the
Jesus of history and the Christ of faith. The church
began to use the weapons of its rationalist enemy to
prove that it was right. Modernism at the beginning of
this century was in fact opposition to such a domestic-
ation by the church of the historical method: people
wanted to give 'scientific' legitimation to an authority
which had gone wrong on a social and political level.

The whole of the polemic over the Jesus of history and the kerygmatic Christ or the Jesus of the church's faith was historically less a christological question than a fight against the exclusivist patent of scriptural interpretation.

So despite all the one-sidedness of Rudolf Bultmann's position we may not forget too quickly the grain of truth in his basic intuition, namely his denial of a smooth continuity between the historical Jesus and the Christ of the church's faith. In the present situation of the churches, who use historical studies about Jesus of Nazareth apologetically in order to demonstrate the continuity between the Jesus of history and the Christ of faith, Bultmann continues to fulfil a critical role over against the belief of the church in a new way. We are all beginning to see more sharply that the historical method is free and independent of any external intervention that is alien to it. And for the churches, on the other hand, this means that for their witness they have no other authority than their own kerygma and that this witness must not therefore be measured by the autonomous, scientific historical method. For Bultmann Jesus Christ belongs in the innermost heart of a church family; he is its inestimable worth. Bultmann was certainly on the track of a correct insight there. However, the retort is, Does this not declare the proclamation of faith 'immune'? Does not a Christian cosiness also have enormous disadvantages?

The 'break', or better the 'striking difference', between the Jesus of history and the Christ of faith is not only a 'modern' question but finds its basis actually in the text of the New Testament. The historical dispute between 'scientific interpretation of the Bible' and 'the church's interpretation of the Bible' has exposed a fundamental theological 'christological problem', namely that the historical figure of Jesus of Nazareth

is in no sense homogeneous with his identity as this was
put into words in and through the church's proclamation and dogmatics. It is evident from church history
that every period makes its own picture of Jesus. It
therefore seems possible to 'manipulate' Jesus by diver-
gent human needs and interests. To mock this fact
involves the risk that one overlooks or indeed ridicules
the at least fourfold difference in the Gospel story of
Jesus's career, or displays a concern to monopolize or
'tailor' Jesus, reducing him to what the French Catholic
theologian Duquoc calls 'an official Vulgate'; in other
words only this one legitimate interpretation of Jesus –
and no other interpretation – is allowed (which is in
contradiction to the New Testament).

Precisely what historical studies have discovered
about the New Testament literature has fundamental
significance for any christology. Speculative theories
about 'christology from above' and 'christology from
below' overlook the real problem which is involved
here; there is often shadow-boxing with an accumu-
lation of all kinds of mutual misunderstandings. Historical studies have made it clear to us that there is no
smooth continuity between the Jesus of history and the
Christ of faith. On the other hand the affirmation of
the identity between Jesus and the kerygmatic Christ is
a basic position of the whole of the New Testament.
Identity and 'diversity' show that the biblical narrative
contains possibilities and perspectives which only
emerge thanks to the mediation of contemporary challenges; the multiplicity of pictures of Christ is essential
for the figure of Jesus of Nazareth as the biblical narrative depicts him. Jesus is indeed a historical and therefore contingent being; his historical career must explain
the biblical expectations and his honorific titles and not
vice versa. We see this latter development taking place
in the New Testament. It is not the case that Jesus

simply illustrates or embodies in concrete terms the religious ideas and conceptions already present in his time in his Jewish tradition. In that case there would indeed be no originality in Jesus; in that case too Jesus would be stuck in one interpretation. The particular event of Jesus of Nazareth interprets what Messiah, Son of God, Lord means, and these titles are not interpretations of Jesus, as is often thought. We do not know in advance what Son of God means when applied to Jesus; even the fact that Israel's king and Israel itself are called Son of God cannot tell us in what sense Jesus can and must be called Son of God. Jesus' own career must explain what this term or honorific title means. The same is true of the expression 'Jesus is our liberator'. Neither old nor new contents of liberation can be used here unless they are subjected to the criterion of Jesus' career from the biblical narrative.

We can discover the answer to this question from the structure of the New Testament. It becomes clear that the authors of the New Testament put all kinds of words into the mouth of Jesus that historically he never spoke. They apply what Jesus said or did creatively to new situations which Jesus did not and could not know in his days in Palestine. They acted in this way, rightly because they were convinced that Jesus himself, who in the Christian conviction of faith had been taken up to the Father after his death, was speaking in the present to believers who lived in quite a different situation from that of the first disciples in Jesus' time. Believers began from the fact that what Jesus had said in quite definite, particular situations retained its meaning even now in other specific situations. The 'universal significance' of Jesus' message which is affirmed in particular situations therefore of course requires to be made a reality ('actualized') in changed circumstances.

With its variety of believing subjects the church com-

munity is the vehicle of this actualization: it knows that
Jesus lives in his church through the gift of the Spirit.
This actualization in faith, even reorientation, in no
way obliterates the historical memory of what Jesus had
said and done. The church community alive today bears
witness to the living actuality here and now of Jesus'
gospel, which found its definitive account in scripture.
Thus scripture remains the necessary reference text,
but the church communities make the text a living word
here and now on the basis of the dialectic that is
maintained between the New Testament story of Jesus'
career, of his death and resurrection on the one hand
and the life of his Spirit in the church of today on the
other. Therefore at least *qua* Christians we cannot make
meaningful statements about God without christology
nor can we make meaningful statements about christology without pneumatology: God, Jesus the Christ and
the Spirit are indissolubly bound together in the Christian understanding of God and of salvation from God.
And at least Christian talk about both christology and
pneumatology is impossible without a living church
community, and is therefore impossible without at least
an implicit ecclesiology. But although for Christians
God and Christ, Spirit and church, are closely connected, we cannot identify all these factors without further
ado.

The church as a visible community of faith arises as
a community of people who stand in the tradition of
Israel and Jesus of Nazareth and who on the basis of
this confess the same faith, celebrate this community
and finally allow their behaviour to be determined by
the guideline of the praxis of the kingdom of God, a
kingdom of justice and love among all human beings
who find their salvation in God: a community of people
of God gathered round the God of people as he is
revealed in Jesus Christ. In this respect the essential

41

feature of the Christian revelation lies in the fact that on the basis of their experience of being with Jesus his followers affirmed that in this man, in his life and message, in his activities and the way in which he died, in his whole person as a man, God's purposes with humanity – and thus the very character of God – were revealed, brought to human awareness in the highest degree. According to this experience of faith Jesus is the place where God has revealed himself in a decisive way as salvation of and for human beings. Christians experience Jesus as the supreme concentration of divine revelation in a whole history of experiences of revelation. In this religious history of revelation human experience has its own irreplaceable place; but, as in any experience of revelation, including 'secular' experience, revelation here is not the fruit of experience, but experience is the fruit of revelation. So this revelation event says something about the self-understanding of particular people and at the same time in talking about their experience these believers do not just want to say something about themselves, i.e. about their life-renewing experience and new understanding, specifically how they see Jesus, but in the first place also something about Jesus himself: that he is the supreme expression of God and that precisely for this reason they have experienced and continue to experience salvation in him. So the expression of faith in no way lays the foundation for revelation by its own intrinsic correctness; rather, revelation itself evokes and provides a basis for the answer of faith by its own power. Certainly good reasons could be given to indicate that to some degree it is not men and women who make God speak but that God makes himself known in and through human experiences as the one who transcends all closely described experiences, and to indicate how he does so.

It is evident from these brief comments that scripture

42

itself therefore provides the proof that the Christian revelation cannot come to us without the mediation of the church. The actual presence of the church in what goes on here and now in the world – the situation (and things and events are not what they were in Jesus' time, indeed the situation is incomparably different) – is therefore the necessary mediation of the actuality and fruitfulness of the gospel of Christ here and now.

But to establish that the church is a necessary mediator in the actualization of Christian faith is in no way to argue for ecclesiocentrism or for putting the teaching office exclusively in the centre of the church. The whole of the living community of the church as it confesses, prays and acts is the subject of this mediation. Moreover, there is a quite tangible difference between the unique situation of the earliest Christian communities and the situation of the post-scriptural church (of both its leaders and the community as a whole). Now as then the church is certainly a *sequela Jesu,* i.e. a community of believers who follow Jesus, and here in the footsteps of Jesus it is visibly and tangibly a social and historical sign of liberation. But it no longer produces new Gospels. The evangelical, apostolic witness in scripture has a uniqueness which the creative witness of contemporary church communities in contemporary situations certainly do not have. The mediation of the church now is thus tangibly different from what it was then. This should never be forgotten, above all by a Catholic ecclesiology, which is often almost exclusively based on papal and episcopal authority. The relationship of the earliest church to scripture is different from the relationship between contemporary churches and this same scripture. Scripture continues to determine all the churches within the earthly sphere of the world of our human history, in which these churches also live. The reference to the Spirit is at the same time a

43

reference to the mediation of the whole of the believing community of the church: it is in no way exclusively an appeal to authority or, on the other hand, to an internalized individual charisma of the Spirit. And that reference to the Spirit, at work in the church community, is at the same time a reference to scripture. Here an unavoidable dialectic comes into play.

The church as ecumene

So churches are not the mystery of God's presence in the world, for this saving presence precedes all the churches. In the language of the reality of salvation the church takes second place: it is the mystery of the *manifestation* of and *confession concerning* God's effective presence in the human world. The church is a sign of God's liberating presence among the nations. Recently, at least within circles in the Roman Catholic church, there has been much misuse of the justified insight that the church is a mystery. But church community as a mystery cannot be found behind or above reality as it is concretely visible. One can define the church in an idealistic way, but if one does one must then keep silent about its relation to history and it is this that marks the churches out as a contingent event in our history. We may not identify the existing churches with the kingdom of God. We need only look at real history to see that no single church is one, holy, catholic, and is only apostolic. The four so-called marks of the church from the Council of Constantinople (384) do not therefore seek to *describe* a reality but are an eschatological call to all churches for repentance. This is the *performative* language of faith.

From the moment that any church concedes its own limitations and opens itself to communion with other churches the pluralism of the Christian churches becomes a positive fact and no longer a Christianity that is torn apart. In that case plurality becomes the empirical condition of the mutual communion of all Christian churches. That is also as it was in the early church:

> As this broken bread was scattered upon the mountains, but was brought together and became one, so let the church be gathered together from the ends of the earth into thy kingdom. For thine is the glory and the power through Jesus Christ for ever. Amen.
> (*Didache*, IX, second century).

Conclusion

At present the ecumene, too, is in a christological crisis. We may not apply without major qualification what I have said about the unity in tension between Jesus of Nazareth and the Christ of faith to another relationship, namely that between the New Testament's, i.e. the church's, Christ and the figure of Christ portrayed by the great councils in the fourth and fifth centuries. Here circumstances are different, because the concept of God in these councils is different from that in the Old and New Testaments. In them we have a Greek concept of God which does not stand in any direct relationship to our earthly time and space. There, too, a quite different image of humanity is used from that in the Bible. Within this conceptual framework of humanity and God (which need to be criticized in the light of the Bible) these councils, precisely in order to remain faithful in a Hellenistic milieu to the New Testament Jesus Christ, were obliged to speak as they did. Authentic Christians were speaking here – but at the same time they were thinking Greeks. What they did secured and saved the New Testament confession for us. But this does not mean that we must accept the philosophical and anthropological presuppositions of these Greek councils (or a particular model of the incarnation) as the condition for a living and unabbreviated faith in Jesus confessed as the Christ. These councils, from Nicaea to Chalcedon, show us little of the vulnerable man Jesus who also suffered on the cross. In these councils the individual Jew Jesus of Nazareth faded away to give place to the 'one human nature', ahistorical. Moreover what these councils meant to say was essentially hardened and often distorted in catechesis, preaching and theology. And in church tradition they often functioned as a source of understanding faith almost independent of the New Testament, standing by themselves: they were even used as a more important source than scripture. The crisis in which many contemporary christologies find themselves today seems to me to lie in the fact that for modern men and women the Chalcedon model no longer speaks in human terms and is usually incomprehensible, while as yet there are no new theological models to make clear today the deepest meaning of Chalcedon. Hence all the searching and experimentation in contemporary christology. We cannot begrudge these seeking Christians time to become clear about Jesus, confessed as the Christ, God's only Son, our Lord.

4

Jesus as the question of men and women to God: mysticism, ethics and politics

The visible community of the church of Jesus the Christ, about which we were thinking in the previous chapter, arose as a community of people who stand in the tradition of the world religions, of Israel and Jesus of Nazareth, and who on the basis of this confess the same faith, celebrate this community, bear witness to it and finally allow their everyday behaviour to be governed by the criterion of the praxis of the kingdom of God: a kingdom of righteousness and love among all men and women who find their salvation in God; a community of 'people of God' gathered round the God of people as he reveals himself in Jesus Christ. In this chapter I shall be speaking about ethics as a hinge and link between the mystical and the political dimensions of Christian faith and finally asking about the truly evangelical and human right of churches in order also to make official pronouncements in situations of injustice.

(a) Jesus and the ethics of the human world

Experiences subject to the criticism of stories of suffering

Although in any human life there are many experiences of meaning, it is nevertheless above all experiences of

47

meaninglessness, of injustice and innocent suffering
which *a priori* have a revelatory significance. It is a fact
that both everyday and scientific experimental experiences owe much to unexpected happenings: to experiences of resistance and the intractability of the reality
in which we live. People live by guesswork and mistakes,
by projects and constructs and therefore by trial and
error; their projects can constantly be thwarted by the
opposition of reality which does not always give itself
to rational human anticipation. Where reality offers
resistance to human plans and thus directs and guides
them in an imperceptible way, we are in contact with a
reality which is independent of us. As I have already
said above, we see that truth comes to us through the
alienation and disintegration of what we have already
achieved and of our plans. It is not the obviousness but
'the scandal' of refractory reality which thus becomes
the principle for the interpretation of reality. The
authority of experiences therefore culminates in stories
of human suffering: stories of pain and misfortunes and
failures, suffering in pain, suffering in evil and injustice,
suffering from and in love, suffering over guilt. Here
are the great elements of the revelation of reality in
and through finite human experiences. For experiences
which resist the subject of the experience, and in
extreme cases the whole of his or her environment and
society, only help us human beings to make authentic
progress. The deepest experiences which guide and
support our life are, moreover, experiences of conver-
sion, crucifying experiences which evoke *metanoia*, a
change of mind, of action and being. Such experiences
demolish their own given identity, but do so in order
to lead to a new integration, to a better identity.

We have experiences within a horizon of experience,
within a searchlight. The searchlight of the Christian
tradition of experience does not just have as its content

an intention to liberate humanity and thus have an emancipatory significance; however, it is not just meant to be semi-emancipation which has no eye for the suffering in human history that has already taken place or for the suffering of others, no eye for the dead. Is there also a future for the dead? Here pure emancipation has nothing to say.

Earlier, and also contemporary, forms of ethics begin – and began – from the natural law or from the ordinances of creation. They presuppose that 'order' is given and that a commandment arises out of it, not to disrupt the order. Here we have a degree of optimism about the interpretative power of 'universal' human reason. That this abstract universal reason (celebrated by the Enlightenment) is itself also entangled in personal and social sinfulness and an avaricious lust for power is often forgotten. At any rate experience teaches that even moral reason needs liberation. If we look more closely we see that the concrete starting point of ethics is not so much 'order' which is not to be disrupted but our indignation over specific historical human beings who are already being hurt everywhere, over the lack of order both in our own heart and in society and its institutions. The actual threat to and attack on the *humanum* which is desired but never capable of positive definition leads to indignation and is therefore a specific ethical challenge and an ethical imperative, therefore embedded in very situational negative experiences of contrast of human disaster and unhappiness, here and now.

So what is ethically good will only emerge, in this view, in a praxis of liberation and reconciliation. Both believers and non-believers have these protesting experiences of contrast. In an autonomous ethic, an ethic without belief in God, there is clearly some desperate concern for a certain utopia which at least does not

49

want complicity in the injustice and lack of freedom which extends over our world. No single religious tradition can of course be reduced to its ethics. One can even say of the Christian tradition that the specific character of the ethics of Christians (as opposed to some other religion, e.g. Islam) lies in the fact that it has no ethics of its own and is therefore open to the *humanum* which is sought by all men and women, here and now and ever anew. This autonomy is already defended by Thomas Aquinas (*Summa Theologiae* I-II, q.107 a.4). We do not need God as a direct foundation for our ethical action. Morality with an autonomous basis is concerned with the human value of each individual *etsi deus non daretur*. And here in the first place collective humanity itself has a responsible claim of its own.

Nevertheless this does not get rid of God from ethical life !

Ethics and belief in God

Although religion cannot be reduced to ethics, on the other hand there is an intrinsic connection between faith and ethics. The Christian sees the autonomous morality of humanity concretely in the context of a practice in accord with the kingdom of God on which he or she has set his or her hope. The spirituality of the ethics of Christians, which as ethics really does not add anything to an autonomous reality focussed on men and women and their worth, lies in theologal life: in a warm relationship with God; life in faith, hope and love which is celebrated in the liturgy, meditated on critically in faith in contemplation and practised in the everyday life of Christians. Ethics which in this way (despite its relative autonomy) is anchored in belief in God is supported by a realistic hope for a God who acts in our history for the liberation of humanity in our society.

This ethics, directly founded on human worth, autonomous, but ultimately nevertheless rooted in God,
finds its basis in the acceptance of humanity by God =
(*iustificatio*) and therefore in the complete liberation of
human beings by God. The old principle of 'acting in
accordance with reason' does not therefore collapse
here; it keeps its force and validity, but gets another
context: between the impulse of belief in God (liberation
faith as concern for our fellow men and women, solidarity with each fellow human being) and ethical action
is the mediation and the criterion of moral reason
which also protects our action in faith from religious
fanaticism. The starting point of ethics in the Christian
religious perspective is not, however, (unfree) universal
moral reason (which is often at work to the disadvantage
of the 'insignificant') but belief in God which leads to
a historical enterprise of a human praxis of liberation
and provokes reflection. In that case practical moral
reason with its demand for rationality is subject to the
stimulating criticism of the human history of innocent
suffering and injustice, of stories of suffering which
have no rational explanation. The Christian gospel in
particular lives by the critical recollection of the human
history of suffering; it recalls the message and praxis of
Jesus, who went to the poor and the oppressed and
therefore also himself experienced suffering and a martyr's death. In its micro- and macro-ethical dimensions,
for believers (even if they do the same as non-believers)
ethical life is the recognizable content of faith, the
historically consistent manifestation or the becoming
transparent of the approaching kingdom of God in
fragments of our human history. The religious, or faith,
is not the ethical. However, faith manifests itself not
only in prayer, liturgy and ritual but also in human
ethics as the side of theologal life which frees men and
women and makes them happy and, at the same time,

51

as the visible touchstone of the truth of faith, prayer
and celebration, which, separated from that, can begin
to lead a life of its own in a neutral, uncommitted
relationship without personal and political ethical impli-
cations. What is decisive is the praxis of the kingdom
of God in solidarity with all men and women and,
moreover, precisely in that and as a result of it, in a
partisan choice for the poor and oppressed, against the
oppression of powerful people and structures which
grind down men and women. The question of the
historical identity of the Christian tradition of experience and the possibilities of handing it on is not about
what Christians can still say and do over and above what
is already said and done by men and women, thinking and acting honestly, who are concerned about the
threats to humanity. Rather, it is a matter of the
whole breadth, depth and height of the critical and
liberating potential for action in Christian hope.

Ethics is a form of self-obligation: people autonomously
impose a norm on themselves. This is a gain in human
insight above all since, and thanks to, Kant. But without
the spirituality of the believer or theologal life purely
human ethics often makes excessive demands on human
beings. Ethics without theologal spirituality often then
becomes 'graceless' in the twofold meaning of the word.
In that case there is ethics without the element of love
which brings happiness, in which love of God and love
of humanity are one and the same indivisible basic
attitude or virtue. From a Christian point of view love
of humankind is itself at the same time a divine virtue,
a reflection of God's love for humanity in concrete
human action. Without spirituality or a perspective on
God in faith ethics is often graceless: eager for ven-
geance and retribution – where Christians speak of
compassion and reconciliation. Although ethics is poss-

ible before any religious confession of faith, ethical competence nevertheless presupposes God's grace and thus theologal life as a living response to this grace. This last finally gives us moral capacity, to the point of death. At any rate it is a matter of human freedom which becomes ethically effective, not of a bourgeois freedom, i.e. my freedom if need be at the expense of the other person. Christian, evangelical freedom is freedom in solidarity, in which the freedom of the one does not become a threat to the freedom of another, as was often the case – and still is – with the liberal bourgeois freedoms, and also with communist freedoms. Evangelical freedom can only be liberated freedom, a freedom released from egoism and power, a freedom which rests on the acceptance of everyone by God even before men and women begin to act. Our God is a God who accepts people beyond the limits of their ethical capacity and actions and regardless of the broken status of their concrete humanity. He is therefore a God of liberation, forgiveness and reconciliation, without which any ethics, whether personal or socio-political, can become fatally graceless, often fanatical and degrading to humanity. Ethics needs a God who is more than ethics. The more we are silent about and even ignore this God who is 'above ethics', the ultimate source of all ethics, the more we human beings deliver ourselves into the hands of idols or self-made gods, to a belief which results not in life but in the torture and death of many. Precisely because God competes with our idols and in this respect is a 'jealous' God, he proves to be a God of human beings, our God whose honour never conflicts with our humanity, but on the contrary respects it and elevates it.

Some people ask whether we need God for ethics and

thus for the human work of peace, humanization and liberation. Do not e.g. agnostics, non-believers, do the same thing – sometimes even better?

That is a serious question, but the question to be put in reply is, 'need which God?' Moreover, what do you mean by 'need'? Certainly not a God as God of the gaps. Nor a God who as a tyrannical potentate arbitrarily imposes his will and law on people, as though (even for God) not the human but God was the direct foundation of ethical obligation. And certainly not a God to whom human beings appeal when their ethical arguments become shaky and who resort to the will of God in order to fill in the gap in those arguments. God will not allow himself to be misused in this way. Believers from many religions have all too often misused the name and will of God in their ethics and above all in their concrete ethos and thus embittered human beings, their human worth and happiness, enslaved and dishonoured them, and laid burdens upon them – particularly on women – which have nothing to do with the will of God. In that case it is better nowadays not to believe in 'God' than to think in terms of an inhuman God who enslaves men and women and then go on to talk about radicalism. Here we in no way have a nineteenth-century belief in progress or the pressure of a permissive society. What is at stake is the nature of the God of Christians: his honour and our honour 'to be able to be human' thanks to God's beloved creation. Older religions with an inhuman God incorporated in their confession (one who, for example, calls for human sacrifice) have all rapidly died away; they cannot withstand human (and thank God also religious) pride 'in being human' despite all human misery. But even religions which in their confessions do not revere an inhuman God but one concerned for humanity can become incredible because of the specific form of their proclamation; in so doing they marginalize many believers from their community of faith. These often bid farewell to their church with honest regret in their heart, but they do not leave their religious tradition of experience. True happiness also knows the cross and can withstand abuse. But here 'the cross' is not cherished, not even by God as a redemptive event posited in principle. Human beings, not God, brought Jesus to the cross, although God could not be checkmated by this. We certainly need no divine grandfather, a kind soul to whitewash and make light of our mistakes and our cowardice. We need deep concern for humanity and thus 'need' a God who is pure freedom, unmerited, generously given grace.

For the Christian tradition of experience only a God of life and not a God of life and death, only a living God – a God of living and dead who still have a future in him – can be worshipped, revered and celebrated by men and women; not a God who humiliates and hurts them or holds them down and denies them joy, and only he has a prophetic liberating force – critical of humanity and society – which thanks to the doxological spirituality of the theologal life of believers reveals itself in life in accordance with the gospel, the practice of an ethics which is both personally and politically liberating and has a basis in prayer or mysticism.

The mystical-theologal dimension of the ethical action of Christians

Certainly in modern times the universal human experience of the ethical demand, not as an abstract principle but as the reality of the other person in need which challenges me, summons me and makes demands on my freedom, has been noted as a privileged place where it is possible to identify a meaningful experience of God.

E.Levinas (*Totalité et Infini*, The Hague 1961) in particular has analysed this phenomenon. The appearance or epiphany of 'the other' breaks the claims of my totality and my I-relatedness: the other is really other, transcendent. 'Receiving and encountering the other puts my freedom in question' (op.cit., 58). So there is a priority of ethical demand over religious appeal. A religion which enslaves or disheartens men and women is by definition a false belief in God or at least a religion which misinterprets itself and has lost contact with its own authentic roots. What comes first is the other person's face as an ethical challenge to my free subjectivity. In our experiences there is a dimension which breaks through all totalitarian demands of the empirical sciences, viz. the ethical experience of the underivable demand which the other person makes on me. To encounter the other in an ethical way is in no way to encounter him or her as an *alter ego* according to the Kantian demand: 'Do not do to others what you do not want to have done to you' (the logic of fair play from the bourgeois Enlightenment), far less to encounter him or her as an element of a totality (member of a state, of a society, or of the human race). It is in fact to encounter the other as an originally unique transcendent other to whom I am related in an asymmetrical relationship (op.cit., 51, 201). In other words I can encounter the other person as someone whose existence can make demands on me, demands which cannot be derived from the moral demands that I can make on him or her. Beyond question I can go on to generalize this absolute demand of the other person in his or her transcendent otherness at a later stage into an ethical principle and draw from that the conclusion that he or she is also required not to hurt me, as Kant did. But the principle that the innocent other may not be hurt is based on the underivable concrete phenomenon of personal otherness and I can adapt this principle to serve my own interests only because I can also be this unique 'other' for others. Levinas acutely arrives at the insight that what the other person can demand of me is not a consequence of what I can demand of him or her. The ethical personhood of the other person is in a kind of non-reciprocal real relationship to me, unlike the relationship between my personhood and the other.

There is something special in the relationship between the other person's freedom and my own. I have said that this relationship is ethically asymmetrical. The other is transcendent not because he or she should be as free as I am. His or her freedom enjoys a superiority which arises out of their transcendence (op.cit., 53). Here Levinas is reacting against the I-relatedness of the Sartrean *pour soi* (the I). The other imposes himself or herself as a demand which dominates my freedom and therefore as more original than anything that takes place in me. 'The other, whose exceptional presence comes to crystallization in the ethical impossibility of killing him or her which I experience. That I no longer have any power over him or her shows that he or she completely transforms any idea that I can have of him or her' (op.cit., 201). This is the opposite of the modern bourgeois freedom which has existed since the Cartesian ego with its *cogito* that posits itself in a sovereign way independently of 'the other'.

The priority of the ethical then means that there can be no knowledge of God without social relationships. For Levinas the other is not a mediation, not an incarnation of God, but through the distinctive features of his or her face he or she is the manifestation of the place where God reveals himself (op.cit., 59). And he concludes from this that what cannot be derived from an interpersonal relationship is in the last resort a primitive form of religion: 'le face-à-face demeure situation ultime' (op.cit., 59).

But from a Christian perspective this view of Levinas leads into a morass or an aporia. The other is not only the origin of an ethical claim on me; he is often also possible violence and injustice, as I am for him. In order to rescue the meaning of the ethical demand I must therefore accept that it is worth the trouble, indeed that it is my ethical duty, to heed the ethical demand of justice and recognize the other even if the other is in fact the source of injustice and violence. Here an inspiration of Kant is rightly taken up: if only human beings, only the other, are a source of value and meaning (as Levinas says), then there is no guarantee that evil will not have the last word over our existence as ethically responsible beings. To suppose that men and women are the only and ultimate source of ethics therefore leads to an aporia. And this is above all the case if one thinks in terms of an asymmetrical ethical relationship between the other and my freedom: the other is always also the one who poses a constant threat, the possible source of injustice.

A fairly dramatic example can illustrate what I mean. Suppose that a young soldier in a dictatorship is told on penalty of death to shoot dead an innocent hostage, purely and simply because the hostage is, for example, a Jew, a Communist or a Christian. The soldier refuses to carry out the order on grounds of conscience. He is certain that he himself will be shot along with this hostage (who in any case will be shot by someone else). In this refusal the soldier recognizes in the humiliated bewilderment of the hostage an unexpressed and perhaps inexpressible moral summons which he experiences as a demand. The other makes a demand on his freedom; he finds it ethically impossible to kill him and therefore refuses to carry out the order.

In this act of conscience which on the one hand points to 'the end of the powers' through the disarming act of the soldier there is, on the other hand, something paradoxical, even bordering on the absurd. For the moral gesture of the soldier is both ineffective as far as the life of the hostage is concerned (he will be shot by someone else) and moreover directly destructive of his own life with all its possibilities which have not been realized (he too will be shot dead). The soldier therefore seems to have had an ethical demand put on him, to make a gesture the absurdity of which cannot be disguised. Precisely that is the reason why other people in such situations take refuge in utilitarian and pragmatic solutions, or favour suicide.

Thus the other who makes an ethical demand on me leads on the one hand to an aporia: that there is no guarantee that evil – violence and injustice, torture and death – will not have the last word over our finite experiences in the world, and on the other to a degree of absurdity: the evidently useless gesture which seems to benefit nobody. Here two ethically honest 'solutions' are possible. On the one hand an appeal to the 'heroic action', which is how Sartre or Camus would judge this case: a heroic gratuitous action on behalf of the *humanum*. On the other hand in the direction of a religious answer, albeit at the same time on behalf of the *humanum*. Both solutions evoke a vision of reality in which by dedication to the *humanum* – the specific person in his or her integrity – human beings become the victims of the power of facts as they empirically are, but as a result at the same time put empirical factuality 'to shame'. Because of someone's positive answer to another's ethical interpellation, despite all appearances, the gratuitous act celebrates a victory over the ultimate triumph of factuality. In both cases we have the hope of the ultimate victory of good: faith in humanity despite everything.

But in that case the question arises on what this hope is grounded. What are the theoretical truth-conditions for it? In the religious answer God himself is the ground of this hope and there are grounds for hope. But what are the grounds for the non-religious, humanistic belief in the ultimate victory of the good over the apparent empirical triumph of actual evil? Is this only a postulatory hope, i.e. a hope against all hope posited in a positivistic way by our free will? This can certainly be courageous and gallant, but at the same time is it not wishful thinking? Belief in humanity despite everything can be a positivistic act of will, since in that case people want to pull themselves out of the morass by their own bootstraps. A total emancipatory self-liberation is contradicted by the fact that human beings are not only a source of grace for their fellow men and women but also a threat, a source of violence and annihilation, time and again, with increasingly refined technical means. To say that martyrdom is not vain and that coming generations will hear of the story and will reap the fruits of previous suffering may be true for many or some people. But the case of the soldier can often be repeated in the future. And it is repeated. So one can in fact interpret the refusal of the soldier in a secular sense as a prophetic action in the hope of the ultimate triumph of humanity, but in that case one must be well aware that there is no anthropological historical basis for this hope. Is it a postulatory hope? Not that such a hope can have no social and historical effects for good. The bold action of the soldier is in a position to articulate the aspirations of an important section of people in society.

But one should not make too absolute a contrast between the humanistic-agnostic and the religious interpretations of this martyrdom. The humanistic hope is not merely postulatory: it has a basis in an autonomous ethical conviction. At any rate one can suppose that there is hope for the triumph of the human because the sacrifice of this soldier recognizes the justice on his own side, and not as seen by the authority. The human conviction of the rightness of justice as opposed to injustice indeed remains a ground for hope. Of course this human conviction is just as present among believers and is in fact the worldly mediation of their faith in God. Religious and agnostic, humanistic people continue to trust that justice is right rather than injustice and evil. The agnostic, even militantly atheistic J.-P. Sartre said on his death bed: 'And yet I continue to trust in the humanity of humankind.' Humanistic hope is not purely postulatory; the conviction that one is on the side of the right gives a reason for this expectation; hope is grounded on the rightness of justice, despite the fact that the world as we experience it constantly contradicts this right empirically.

The humanist certainly does not know in the end whether reality will prove this ethical conviction of standing on the side of justice to be right. The great difference from the religious view is therefore that a hope with a purely autonomous foundation in ethics does offer a perspective on a perhaps better humanity for some or many people in the future, but forgets the many sacrifices that have been made and the many victims that have still to fall. The fallen themselves do not experience any liberation or redemption; they have lived so that in the future perhaps some people should not have to suffer the same fate. In the religious experience of this extreme, intensely ethical situation the believer sees and experiences reality in its absolute limits at the deepest level not as blind fate, not as wild chance, but in fact as personal, namely as supported by God's absolute saving presence which is near to us in

61

situations which he did not want, did not even tolerate, but in fact are absurd. The absurd is not argued away, far less understood rationally or given religious approval, but it is not the last word for believers: believers entrust the absurdity to God who is the source of pure positivity and the transcendent foundation of all ethics, the mystical ground of all ethical commitment, as a result of which there is still hope for the victim himself, who outside the religious perspective is written off for good. It is not that the martyr does his courageous deed in order to obtain an eternal reward. Certainly his or her historical deed is itself stronger than death. The believer sees faith that what is just and good is right, rather than injustice, as an experience of the *metahumanum* (for people evidently cannot achieve this in their history), especially of the absolute presence of God's pure positivity in the historical mixture of meaning and meaninglessness that make up the phenomenon of humanity and our history. This is not to belittle humanity by a Christian reference to a completely alien element, God. For this reference to God on the one hand is mediated by the human conviction of the human rightness of justice as opposed to all injustice and on the other is a reference precisely not to a completely alien source, but to the ultimate, innermost source of all justice: the intimate presence of the exclusively positive reality, 'God': a God who wills not death but life for his own, for all. Here there is an evocative expression of the fact that for those who believe in God, above all Christians, religion, belief in God, in one and the same movement frees human beings for love of God and for love of fellow human beings and above all for love for the ill-treated and outcast (Matt.25.40).

In sacrifice for fellow human beings, up to and including ethical martyr deaths, we have a tangible human context within which (in a massively secular world) a humanly relevant and philosophically meaningful notion of God can be introduced that opens up a distinctive comprehensibility which others can understand. In this way we get insight into the religious point of reference, God, the other, to whom we stand in a theologal but essentially also really asymmetrical ethical relationship. Both the humanistic secular and the religious answer thus lies in a 'vain – superfluous – sacrifice', whether in a heroic sense or as a 'vain sacrifice of love' in a deeply human sense of holy, non-heroic trust in God despite everything. These are two possibilities of human life which are intrinsically capable of being understood rationally. For the believer the religious interpretation is more easily understood and more reasonable; the non-believer finds the agnostic interpretation more reasonable. But in this context what believers mean by God can also be understood by non-believers. The believer has sufficient token of this belief in his human experience and without losing the reality of the human character of these experiences.

The most obvious, modern way to God is that of welcoming fellow human beings, both interpersonally and by changing structures which enslave them. Moreover that is not a purely theoretical or speculative approach to God (ontological foundations or decisionistic proclamations of free subjectivity), but a meta-ethical, viz. religious or theologal, interpretation of a micro- and macro-ethical human possibility. It is no metaphysics of being or of free subjectivity, but believing reflection on the praxis of justice and love. What we have here is not just the ethical consequence of religious or theologal life; here ethical praxis becomes an essential component of the true knowledge of God: 'He judged the cause of the poor and needy; then it was well. Is not this to know me? says the Lord'(Jer.22.16). God is accessible above all in the praxis of justice: 'No one has ever seen God; if we love one another, God abides in us and his love is perfected in us' (I John 4.12).

Conclusion

Mediated by the human conviction that human beings cannot treat good and evil, justice and injustice on the same footing and that therefore right is on the side of good, belief in God makes the theoretical connection between the human hope of the victory of the *humanum* and the specific reality of our history. The practical mediation between this hope founded on God and the world of historical experience takes place through the action of those who believe in God in changing and improving the world, while at the same time we know that where this goes wrong through human injustice, this is not the last word, because the practical mediation is taken up into trust in God whose future for us is greater than our historical future. Thus belief in God is the basis of a world-renewing prophetic praxis. Believing praxis bears the promise of hope. Ultimately (for Christians) historical mediation is achieved through eschatological reminiscence in the death and resurrection of Jesus which is itself a promise that has not yet been fulfilled for humanity, though it nevertheless has a foundation. Thus the hope of believers is dialectically reconciled with the contradiction of the world as they experience it – reconciled, not in an undialectical model of harmony but through the critical and productive, saving practice of living people and through the belief that there is always a surplus of hope over and above the recalcitrant world as we experience it.

For the believer, this surplus of hope over against what has already been realized in history is based on what we call God's creation for the purpose of salvation: God's absolute saving presence in what he has called to life. Precisely this gracious presence, mediated in our experience in and through our essential finitude and through both experiences of meaning and negative experiences of contrast, remains an inexhaustible source of a never-failing potential of expectation in humanity which cannot be secularized. Life without belief in God is not yet the same thing as life in a world from which God's active saving presence had disappeared (though only believers can draw such a distinction). Faith in God is thus both affirmation and criticism, and therefore not merely negative criticism or 'divine proviso'. Precisely because this faith is affirmative, productive or liberating, it also has a critical power which criticizes a lack of freedom and disaster. To claim to know better and to give any positive content to what definitive salvation will be is to run the risk of either human megalomania or a trivialization of God's possibilities.

(*b*) Ethics as a link between the mystical and the political dimensions of Christian belief in God

The theologal-mystical dimension of Christian belief in God

Alongside its ethical, inter-personal, ecological and socio-political dimensions the Christian life of faith also has a mystical dimension, that is, an aspect of cognitive union with God. The character of faith which touches on God is what I call the mystical side of faith. This cognitive dimension of faith has two aspects: the aspect of representations of faith expressed in confessions, concepts or imagery, viz. faith in God, confessed as creator, redeemer or liberator, and the aspect of cognitive contact with the reality of God (a particular mystical tradition in fact speaks of *thigganein*, the Greek word for 'touch, contact'). In that case, mysticism in the more special sense is an intense form of experience of this cognitive element in faith which binds us with God, while the elements of imagination here move right into the background and even disappear completely. Given the unique nature of God who transcends all understanding and experience, mysticism therefore constantly has the element of a 'dark night'. Here we come up against the paradox of both the life of faith and mysticism as an intense form of the life of faith. To believe in God without conceptions of God is senseless and even impossible, and moreover is historically ineffective, whereas on the other hand God's absolute presence leaves all our images and conceptions of God in the lurch again. The Bible, both the first and second Testaments, is full of images of God and at the same time full of the shattering of ideas of God. Therefore I must first go rather more deeply into this paradox of faith, which is also the paradox of all mysticism.

Basically we are dealing here with God's grace, i.e. with the saving and real presence of God among us; this is not a separate sector, e.g. of human inwardness, but embraces the whole reality in which we live and of which we are a part. From God's side this absolute nearness is immediate; for us this immediacy is mediated, while it remains immediacy. (I am well aware that this sort of thing is nonsense in terms of interpersonal relationships, but not if it is a matter of a reciprocal relationship between a finite and an infinite being. A reference to 'immediate experiences' can be very misleading!) Therefore in my view the whole problem of mysticism can be summed up in the term 'mediated immediacy' (even if when putting their experiences into words mystics speak of immediacy, their analysis betrays the fact that this immediacy is mediated, above all in John of the Cross and even in Eckhart). Mysticism lies in the extension of prayer: it is a prayer in which an attempt is made to transcend the elements of faith which are also mediated by politics, ethics and conceptuality in order to put oneself directly into the immediate proximity of God. Now because of the distinctive nature of God and the necessarily varied mediation of any belief in God's absolute saving nearness that is never successful and therefore the highest peaks of mysticism show themself as 'dark nights' (John of the Cross), or even more daringly, as 'dark light' (Ruysbroeck). Without mediation mysticism in fact seems to be seeking a void, a *nada*, as John of the Cross puts it, but authentic mysticism involves a *nada* or nothing of overdetermined fullness which cannot be contained in concepts or images – a fullness which, however, can only show itself to the human spirit as such in the form of a dark night or dark light. At this level of mystical prayer there are no longer any positive supports or positive mediations, only the mediation of negativity revealing itself as a black hole or, as Thérèse of Lisieux said, as a wall. Mysticism is a dialogue in which both conversation partners are intensely effective but in which one partner, namely God, seems to be silent, despite all his active involvement.

Mysticism is essentially not just a process of knowledge but a particular way of life – a way of salvation.

Before discussing mysticism as an epistemological problem I must therefore first describe what mystical experiences are. On the basis of descriptions which male and female mystics have given of their mystical way of life I can see here three constants (though with all kinds of differences within each):

1. Mystical experience is a source experience. Among mystics there is an awareness that something fundamental has happened, a sort of sense of enlightenment. In mysticism what used to be the familiar picture of the world and the self (the ego) of the person concerned is radically broken up: his or her old world falls apart and he or she has experienced something completely new, overwhelmingly new, which changes the whole of his or her behaviour. The old words also no longer do; the new experience calls for new words in order to be able to be expressed or articulated. In summary form, there is a kind of breakthrough, a collapse of the old world; the experience of something completely new: light or fire, a glow of love, or '*nada*' or a 'You'. We also find among the mystics paradoxes like 'all' and 'nothing' and indeed find them side by side; what is particularly characteristic is Ruysbroeck's expresssion 'dark light'. There is something transcendent and at the same time all-embracing; the source of both all objectivity and all subjectivity. An unconditional experience of salvation, also an experience of totality, of reconciliation with all things despite the connotation of suffering and lack of reconciliation.

2. A second phase usually follows: the first great sense of love seems to have disappeared; there is gnawing doubt: was it all authentic? There comes what many mystics call the phase of purgation (catharsis) brought about by sharpened concentration; there are also processes of love in terms of what is experienced as 'human wounding', but this does not harm the person but rather exalts him or her. The second phase usually ends up in a night and a wilderness; authentic mysticism is often not fine, but a torment.

3. And yet! In the end mystics discover the features of the countenance of the divine Love, albeit only in

the trace that the beloved has left in the being of the
mystic, man or woman: it remains a mediated immediacy; there is a pure presence of the divine but also the
self-transparent presence of the mystic in God. Mystical
union: mutuality. And yet this happens constantly with
a painful feeling of loss, not seeing.

One can experience this mystical way of life in different contexts and situations. Some have these experiences in and through nature; others like Buber in the
family; others, like Francis, in society and in the world;
others in reading the Torah or scripture or in confront-
ation with Jesus confessed as Christ; others in the experience of the 'you' of the fellow man or woman; others
in turn by sinking into their own being (the so-called
mysticism of being); nowadays for many people it is in
the experience of 'the privilege of the oppressed poor'.
But it is always an experience of totality: a kind of
feeling of the presence of the whole of reality, indeed
an experience of the source of everything. Anyway, the
Inexpressible that is experienced is more real than the
seat on which the mystic sits, more real than what one
usually regards as reality. Mysticism in no way means
'God and only God'. St Francis' hymn to the sun makes
that clear, when Francis says. 'Be praised, my Lord, *with
all your creatures!*' The mystic first of all wants to let
everything go, everything including himself or herself;
but in the grace of God he gets everything back a
hundredfold, himself or herself included. Genuine
mysticism is never a flight from the world, but out of a
first disintegrating source experience arises integrating
and reconciling mercy with everything. It is a resource,
not a flight.

The mediation in any Christian faith, including mysticism, has consequences for the structure of the whole
of faith. Jesus reveals the divinity or the authentic being
of God by revealing him precisely in his friendship

69

towards men and women: as a God concerned with human beings and their humanity. As a result, a concept of God is expressed which is both deeply mystical and prophetic; this happens in an indissoluble unity in which ethics combines the mystical element of faith with the political element of the same faith. This must now be clarified.

The theologal or mystical dimension in political form

Through mediation in faith and mysticism or in the 'theologal' dimension of faith the God of Jews and Christians goes the way of the world and in this sense issues a summons, not to flee from the world but to flee with the world to the kingdom of God, that is, to the anticipation of the kingdom of God in this world; a world made whole, a world as God wants to see it. Here is no contrast between inwardness and outwardness. This is expressed most sharply in the Christian view of love of neighbour and love of God in which Christianity rejects any dualism – as though love of neighbour were subordinate to love of God. There is no question of priorities here. Love of humankind and love of God are one and the same theologal virtue in the Christian tradition; it is the love which comes from God and through the assent of our hearts is taken further towards our fellow men and women. Thus love of humanity as a disinterested commitment for fellow human beings is at the same time the hallmark of the truth of love towards God.

But despite the negation of any dualism, love of neighbour and love of God nevertheless form a unity *in tension*. This tension also becomes visible through and in the distinctiveness of the worldly. For in the love of neighbour love of God is only implicitly, though really, present; on the other hand authentic love of God

70

is implicit love of neighbour. The form of the love of God of the active mystic involved in the world is only implicitly present in his love of neighbour. In the person who prays explicitly this latter is implicitly present. But here it is not a matter of asserting that the one form is better or more perfect than the other; that would be more Hellenism than Christianity, or an expression of modern activism. It does mean that mysticism is possible not just in the form of silence and rest, inwardness and contemplation, but also in the hard and prophetic struggle. On the other hand, by virtue of a distinctive inner dynamics the mystic who is active out of love of humanity has express need of moments of explicit doxology and eucharist, explicit praise and thanksgiving.

In the past, mysticism was often identified with contemplation and, given the historical and social situation, love of neighbour had virtually only the form of inter-personal dealings and encounter. In a modern age, in which we have come to realize that social and political structures (which often hurt people) can also be changed, alongside its other older manifestation love of neighbour also takes the form of political love which, moreover, is supported by the same presence of implicit love of God. So love of God – ultimately mysticism – can enter the concrete social and political commitment of Christians. In that case mysticism and politics are in the same unity in tension for Christians as love of God and love of neighbour, two forms of one and the same theologal attitude. Through this, in our time a field of holiness is opened up which is rightly called 'political holiness' (Jon Sobrino).

Terms like mysticism and political are both ambiguous, even suspect. So let me give a general definition which can be used in a concrete way. I use the term mysticism here to denote an intensive form of experi-

71

ence of God or love of God, and politics to denote an intensive form of social commitment (and thus not the political activity of professional politicians *per se*), a commitment accessible to all people.

I have said that political love is a form of Christian love of neighbour alongside other possible and necessary forms of love of neighbour, like works of charity. But holiness is always contextual; it does not take place in a social vacuum. Given the present situation of suffering humanity which has now been generally recognized, political love can become the historically urgent form of contemporary holiness, the historical imperative of the moment or, in Christian terms, the present *kairos* or moment of grace as an appeal to all believers.

In the Jewish and Christian tradition of faith God is always experienced as a God concerned for humanity who also wants 'people of God' who are concerned for humanity. He is the promoter of good, the opponent of evil. Christian talk about God moreover coincides with talk about the basis of universal hope, talk about God's universal will to salvation in the face of all situations of injustice and thus to the advantage of all people, with a preferential love for those who are farthest removed from salvation, those who are belittled by fellow human beings or by oppressive structures, the poor and downtrodden; the one lost sheep. And there are many of these: the two-thirds of the world's population which is underfed.

Recollection of the life and the execution of Jesus and belief in his resurrection is therefore not just a liturgical action but at the same time a political action. With the Jewish and Christian tradition of faith as a compass, a divining rod or a searchlight, we can test our secular history to see whether it relates to salvation history as God wants it. Precisely in this experience of contrast there is a possibility of a new experience of

72

transcendence. In that case there are two facets in such an experience: (*a*) on the one hand the person, above all the poor and oppressed and all those who have declared themselves to be in solidarity with him or her and act accordingly, experiences that God is absent from many human relationships of possession and power in this world; thus he or she experiences the alienation, the gap, between God, the kingdom of God and our society; (*b*) on the other hand the believer experiences precisely in his or her political love and opposition to injustice an intense contact with God, the presence of the liberating God of Jesus. In modern times authentic faith seems to be nurtured above all in and through a praxis of liberation. In this, awareness grows that God reveals himself as the deepest mystery, the heart and the soul of any truly human liberation. The conceptualization or understanding of that mystery, first veiled in any form of action which truly liberates people, then gets its first explicit expression in words when it is mentioned in the statement of faith, 'You are a liberating God, the Holy One of Israel', not a God of living and dead but a God who wills to give life. The discovery (also made through the searchlight provided by the Jewish-Christian tradition of faith) that God himself is the heart and source of all truly human liberation calls for praise and thanks, for a liturgical celebration of God as liberator, even before we are completely freed and redeemed, for the basis and source of universal hope always precede our action. That was already the story in Israel. And the New Testament picks up this thread of the story.

This form of political love and holiness has its greatest opportunities precisely in our time. Our time as it were summons it up, although we ourselves must interpret this voice; for 'signs of the times' do not speak: we must make them speak. Moreover this political form of the

Christian love of God and neighbour, albeit in another field of experience, knows the same repentance and *metanoia*, the same asceticism and self-emptying, the same suffering and the same dark nights and losing itself in the other as was once the case in contemplative mysticism. This political holiness today already has its own martyrs, for the sake of righteousness among men and women as God's cause; for the mysterious term 'kingdom of God' also denotes that. In the disinterested support of the poor, the oppressed and the outcast as a demand of Christian love precisely in its political and social dimensions there is a severely ascetical process of purification which does not fall short of the ways of purgation in classical mysticism.

That the political sphere as a worldly reality is also full of ambiguity, full of temptations and threats, above all because politics is also concerned with power, cannot be denied. Classical ascetical and mystical love also was and is full of temptations and threats to which many people have succumbed. In fact because of these dangers politics itself calls for holiness and humanization: it must make itself felt as disinterested love. But a praxis of liberation which is supported by political love is, in its emancipation, at the same time (through *metanoia*) a piece of divine redemption. Of course Christian redemption is more than emancipatory self-liberation. But truly human liberation, supported by political love, points in concrete terms to the worldly fruitfulness of Christian redemption. It is an intrinsic ingredient of that. Here experience of God is the ensouling element which goes along with the specific action of liberation in which at the same time this praxis is transcended: it is the active witness to the God of righteousness and love. And because salvation does not coincide completely with our awareness that this salvation comes from God, we may say that wherever good is done and

injustice is challenged, through a praxis based on love
of the fellow human being, the very being of God that
is human love is endorsed and given power. Not 'Lord,
Lord, Alleluia', but praxis is decisive. Without prayer
or mysticism politics soon becomes cruel and barbaric;
without political love, prayer or mysticism soon becomes
sentimental or uncommitted interiority. In an insepar-
able two-in-oneness Christian faith thus has both a
mystical and a political dimension; the bond between
the two is laid by the ethical dimension of Christian
faith.

The political dimension of faith and the official statements of the churches

Roughly speaking one can fairly easily distinguish two
diametrically opposed views among theologians which
leave room for all kinds of intermediate positions.

On the one hand are the advocates of the absolute
neutrality of the church in social and political problems.
These advocates say that the church has no political
competence, that it has no control over secular affairs.
So it must remain politically and socially neutral. Often
they appeal in support of their position to a New Testament saying: 'Render to Caesar the things that are
Caesar's and to God the things that are God's.' As
citizens Christians, like non-believers, are directly or
indirectly involved in politics, but the rule of the autonomy of political reason and politics applies. For a
long time this political liberalism was the hallmark of
Christian progressiveness.

On the other hand at present others regard this first
position, on the basis of a changed society in which the
social dimension has a central place, as the climax of
reactionary conservatism: for many Christians social
and political liberation is an essential dimension of

Christian faith. To liberate people means to bring them to their full truth. Therefore all alienations which hold people captive and oppress them must be unmasked analytically and in practice. To a large degree many (though not all) of these alienations are in fact of a social kind; they are connected with the basic structures of the economic world system in which we live. According to this way of thinking the church. as the bearer of the good news of complete liberation, may not remain neutral towards the problems of world society. If the criticism from the gospel of what the Bible calls 'this wicked world' leaves out of account the social and political structures of this world and thus does not criticize actual injustice in a concrete social order, it is only semi-criticism, a secret understanding with injustice.

Those are the two global tendencies. Moreover within the whole of the latter trend we should also be able to distinguish a significant sub-trend, namely of Christians who begin from the conviction that the only authentic and adequate social criticism is the Marxist analysis of society. They then assert that only a Christianity which is reinterpreted in the light of the Marxist analysis of capitalist society corresponds to the demands of the gospel. I would stress from the start that the second trend may not be identified with this sub-trend. I myself find the resources of the Marxist analysis of society a legitimate possibility, but it is far from being the only possible one or even the best.

The task for us (for me, now, as a Christian theologian) is to combine the spirit of the gospel with political wisdom and thus to honour the truth in the intuition of both views.

To call for the autonomy of political reason (with the representatives of the first trend) seems to me, given the importance of both politics and Christian faith,

completely necessary. Unless they recognize this autonomy Christians soon get caught up in authoritarian
clericalism which claims to know better, the history of
which has shown clearly enough how disastrous it was
and is for both effective civil government of society
and the freedom of the church. Moreover there is no
denying the fact that the Christian revelation does not
give any precise instructions for the economic, social
and political ordering of human society. Those are
matters which belong to the art of government, here
helped by e.g. the political sciences and the lessons of
history.

But it becomes quite a different matter if we were to
conclude from this that the message of the gospel has
nothing to do with the ordering of secular human
society. Love of neighbour, love of God, *caritas* without
justice is a lie; even justice becomes an empty word if
it does not lead to the establishment of a just social and
political order. This calls both for what Paulo Freire
calls conscientization, social awareness, and for the
changing of structures. Therefore (with the representatives of the second trend) we must say that the Christian
message also has political relevance, about which the
churches have a right to speak, namely on the basis of
the insight of faith that the salvation that they claim to
bring also involves the abolition of social and political
alienations. The churches must at all times be ready to
challenge injustice (modestly but dauntlessly); they must
be concerned to further the sense of human solidarity
and social responsibility all over the world.

However, this political relevance of the gospel does
not in any way mean that the churches should take the
government of the world into their hands, nor even
that they should ally themselves with one particular
political and social system. That would be the abolition
of civil political freedom of choice and this is not only

a political but also a moral value, indispensable for the complete exercising of the responsibility which we have for our fellow human beings and for their history (as far as is within our power).

I can see many misunderstandings in the present polemic over these matters (above all that prompted by the book by H.Kuitert, *Everything is Politics, but Politics is not Everything*, SCM Press and Eerdmans 1986). In the strict and technical meaning the term politics relates to specific political practice, that is, the totality of economic, social and political activities, the immediate purpose of which is to call into being a social and political order which is ever juster, ever more human for all people. This does not come about without a power struggle. The citizen who is a Christian and is involved in politics along with fellow citizens who are not believers will find new motives of religious inspiration in the gospel, in his faith, and also extreme sensitivity to the value of the human individual. But this in no way alters the fact that the specific political option is not in any respect a datum of faith; so it does not come under the authority of the church but is something for free citizens to choose freely.

However, political relevance also has a broader general meaning. In that case it means that the nature and the duty of Christian faith and thus also of the official church is to further truth and justice in the world in the way of a spiritual power, critical and ethical, a power which has as its mission keeping alive in the heart of humanity the will to form human society into a *polis*, a city, a dwelling-place in which it is good for everyone to live, something which it is good to live for.

To end these lectures I want to concentrate on the official church, on the church as an institution and on the official statements of the Christian churches on social questions.

As an institution in our society the church itself is *ipso facto* a political factor; by existing as an institution it has an effect on society and its politics. To isolate Christian faith from its involvement with social reality amounts to a loss of its practical relevance for human life. On the contrary, to confuse or identify belief with political commitment or to derive it from that is to lose its own identity. The world is certainly dear to the hearts of Christians, but the hearts of Christians are not set on the world.

According to the distinctive view of faith, too, politics simply has a worldly concern: the aim of politics is the realization of a sphere of life which integrates the basic interests of human life into a rationally ordered whole, and this comprises e.g. control of the natural environment in order to secure the physical survival of humanity; establishing the possibility of intact interactions with the personal environment to realize the social nature of humanity; non-violent ordering of the social sphere which leaves room for the realization of personal human freedom. Here rational human criteria may be that control over the ecological milieu must not pose any threat to the natural basis of human life and that social discrepancies can be tolerated only in so far as they bring the greatest possible advantages to people who are prevented from taking part in social life by disadvantages in their natural or actual social opportunities; that the exercise of power aimed at the maintaining of the internal and external freedom of citizens in society must be endorsed by the free consensus of all involved; finally, that each citizen must have the opportunity to determine his or her own interests without hindrance in so far as these do not damage the fulfilment of the justified interests and needs of others (see e.g. H.-J.Hohn, 'Politischer Glaube?', in *Theologie und Philosophie* 61, 1986, 1-23).

Arguing on this basis I agree with Professor Kuitert that the need for official statements in the political sphere is a service for the church to perform in political emergencies, given the autonomy of political discourse which is also recognized by Christian faith. An 'ayatollahizing' of politics, even in modern dress, translated into Christian terms, comes from the evil one; it makes a farce of both political discourse and Christian belief in God. In all instances in which politics carries out the tasks imposed on it adequately, by any reasonable criteria, there is no reason for the church to make an active intervention. As to content, in any case the church could then say no more or other than what can be found in the newspapers and political journals, and what political parties in fact say and do. Moreover there is no political need and in fact little public interest in a titbit from the church in this area. Before Kuitert is criticized here one must listen well to precisely what he is saying and not wrongly project one's own emotions on to him.

However, as a Christian I have less confidence in this political reason, even within a state system which works in a very democratic way. Not in the first place because of the wickedness of the human heart or the human lust for power, but because of the structural regularities at work in a given system in which implicitly or explicitly the priority is enjoyed by the economy rather than by the *humanum* and political reason. The question is whether the evident emergency situations recognized by Kuitert e.g. in South Africa and Latin America are also connected essentially and structurally with what is going on in our Western democracies and prosperous societies, so that the tensions, e.g., between the north and south axis and the east and west axis, and also the basically cheerless differences throughout the world in the just distribution of material and spiritual goods and work do not make the contemporary political world one great emergency situation over its length and breadth, height and depth. Although as a believer I have confidence in the use of political reason in a democratic system, as a critical believer I must see through the laws by which, in a world system where economic and often also military interests have priority, this political reason is often manipulated and begins to function ideologically. In my view, in specific terms the 'political emergency' is to be found even in the smallest details of the most democratic political decision-making in the West. The pressure of economic processes arising out of what is *de facto* the universal dominance of the economy can make a democratic majority decision a purely ideological decision against which the churches must protest if they still want to be called the church 'of the peace of Christ'. This is not to undermine democracy but to perform a service for true democracy. The churches therefore may and must also be officially active in politics, albeit in their own style – and not as a third or fourth political power block in society, especially when the limits and aims of politics which are established by reason are infringed, i.e. if politics is practised in a totalitarian way or is imposed through violence in areas in which it is not subjected to the laws of what can be established and controlled, or if the historical contingency of political structures is distorted ideologically or if politics becomes 'everything'. In that case it is in the interest of political reason itself for the churches to provide a reminder that it is transgressing its limits or not living up to its task. But in that case it is vital that the churches do not just issue admonitions or give advice but also argue. The burden of proof lies with anyone who does not agree with this. What the churches have to say in the political sphere must be open to discussion on a rational basis. Appeals to Bible and tradition make no sense to the political public. References to the will of God or the ordinances of creation can be justified in the political sphere only if we examine the structures of society to see whether they make possible the furtherance of freedom, honesty and morality. For the Christian message has freed us for freedom, rationality and morality; it has disarmed any attitude which is dictated by anxiety and unreason.

Whether church criticism or political decisions are right must always be clarified by arguments. The churches must only take note of criticism of their political commitment if their arguments are not in fact adequate, or if their activity is preventing or undermining the realization of social freedom and the functioning of democracy. This means that they join in social discussion not with confessions but with arguments.

For me the social and political proclamation of the church is not something separate from its proclamation of faith, even when in this sphere the church must have the courage to speak cautiously and sometimes even hypothetically, and with arguments that are also accessible to non-believers.

Above all, churches can intervene actively in politics when political themes are not purely political – which is often the case – and the question implies 'What kind of humanity are you opting for?' That is clearly the case with legislation about biotechnology, the arms race, peace and so on. In all these questions politics must be open to the wishes and votes of many spheres of society, including religions and churches. One cannot attribute omnipotence and omniscient competence to politics any more than one can attribute these characteristics to the churches in this sphere. What counts is responsible argument which is above all open to discussion, in the sense that secular entities, like political ones, may not be deified, just as the demonizing of all politics is of the evil one. One cannot politicize all problems.

Conclusion

For the churches to talk about politics is inevitably a source of tension within them. However, polarization in the churches must not be seen as the greatest danger to threaten the church. Any statement by the church has polarized the churches, right from the time of the New Testament and all the great ecumenical councils. One cannot preserve unity at the expense of the gospel. Unanimity in church politics as the unity of a sociological group has little to do with the unity for which the Johannine Jesus prayed. And on the other hand the multiplicity of christologies and ethical options which we find in the New Testament is in no way detrimental to the canonical unity which the churches endorse in these writings.

Therefore above all in our days we must look to the massive monolith of dangers which threaten humanity. We can bring together a concerted positive will to reverse these dangers (think only of the arms spiral, national disputes between majorities and minorities, world hunger, the impoverishment of the Third World, unemployment, the rise in racism, the damage to the environment, discrimination against women and minorities, and so on) by action in solidarity. Above all a common concern in solidarity for the poor and oppressed reunites men and women in the 'ecumene of suffering humanity' and this action in solidarity can then bring us back to theory; in other words, through orthopraxis we can again confess and express in new words an authentic and living orthodoxy.

After Auschwitz, Hiroshima, Bergen-Belsen and so on, and the strangulating grasp on our ecological environment (as symbols of what is 'demonic' in our history), one can no longer theologize and make church pronouncements in the same old way. We need a new productive mediation between the gospel and our political sphere.

One important consequence of this is an end to *liberal* pluralism. Negative or far-reaching experiences of contrast compel us to a new, clarity and unanimity, which this time is not fundamentalistic, in place of the old liberal pluralism of many modern theologies, conceptions of faith and forms of church action. Action in solidarity over the dangers that threaten humanity can give us a vision, which is new and yet faithful to the gospel of our fundamental confessions of faith, so that these confessions of faith remain doxological, i.e expressions of praise and thanksgiving, but at the same time open up their political dimension.